MEN Are Like FISH

What Every Woman Needs To Know About Catching A Man

SECOND EDITION

Steve Nakamoto

Java Books

Huntington Beach, California

"Men are Like Fish" and "America's #1 Metaphor For Love" are trademarks of Java Books and Steve Nakamoto.

Published by Java Books
17202 Corbina Lane, Suite 204
Huntington Beach, California 92649
E-mail: menarelikefish@mindspring.com
Phone/Fax: 714-846-0622

For More Information: www.MenAreLikeFish.com

Books may be purchased for educational, business, or sales promotional use. For information, please write: Special Marketing, Java Books, 17202 Corbina Lane, Suite 204, Huntington Beach, CA 92649.

Publisher's Cataloging-in-Publication Data
Nakamoto, Steve.
    Men are like fish: what every woman needs to know about
    catching a man. second edition/Steve Nakamoto. –
    Huntington Beach, California, Java Books, 2002.
        p. cm.
    ISBN 0-9670893-2-8
        1. Relationships. 2. Self-help. 3. Psychology.
        I. Title.
HG567345.R454345   2002   99-53334
658.9   dc—21   CIP

03 02 01 00 ❦ 5 4 3 2 1

Printed in the United States

A Special Note to the Reader

This book is dedicated to helping people make better decisions on how to attract, select, get, and keep more romantic, committed, and fulfilling love relationships through clearer perception and deeper understanding.

On another level, this book is especially dedicated to those gallant women who persist in their noble cause to save decent but unenlightened men from becoming increasingly grumpy, unattractive, stuck-in-their-ways, isolated, socially-lazy, stubborn, old fish that no one can or wants to catch. (While women can often live joyful fulfilling lives without men, the reverse is rarely true.)

And lastly, this book is dedicated to all the wonderful men and women who have endured deep heartache and disappointment, but still move forward in their love lives knowing that the emotional gifts inside their hearts were truly meant to be shared with someone special.

May this book provide you with the proper insights, strategies, tools, and most of all, enlightened spirit.

Disclaimer

Contents

Introduction

During Valentine's Week, I watched the 2001-2002 season's finale of *HBO's* hotter-than-hot Sunday night hit television series, *Sex and the City,* starring Sarah Jessica Parker.

An endorsement for that final episode which appeared in the weekend edition of the *USA Today* prior to its public showing read, "*HBO's Sex and the City* ends its season with a truly lovely salute to missed romantic chances and the indestructible glory of New York. It's the perfect grown-up send-off for the show's most mature season."

As a fan of that popular show, it often occurs to me that in spite of many differences, men and women want essentially the same things out of their love lives. They both dream of having a love relationship with the following key ingredients:

- Driving passion
- Beautiful romance
- Supportive friendship
- Intimate connection
- Outrageous fun
- Personal growth
- Enhanced self-esteem
- Peace of mind

Unfortunately only a few people will ever experience loving relationships that live up to their dreams. Why is that so?

Most people would say it's just a case of bad luck. But I contend that a lack of success over the course of someone's entire life is more a matter of making poor decisions.

For those of you who have tried just about every approach, and still possess the burning desire for a great love life, here's a fresh, innovative angle on how to capture the heart of a good man—an angle that will naturally lead to an exciting, fulfilling, and lasting love relationship.

**"If you continue to think as you've always thought,
you'll continue to do what you've always done,
and you'll continue to get what you've always gotten."**

As a man, I'm certainly not claiming to know how women think and feel. I am also not foolish enough to say that every woman has to catch a man in order to live a happy and fulfilling life. Rather, I am offering you a new twist on the age-old subject of how to make love happen.

You and I both realize that almost everything has already been written (in regards to relationship advice) on the subject of love and romance. So it may not come as a shock to you when I maintain that in most cases "advice" alone won't do much for making your love life any better.

What I believe will dramatically improve things for you, however, is the use of effective thinking tools. The ones that you'll find here will enable you to make smarter decisions concerning what makes you most attractive, how to measure a man's value to you wisely, where to meet the good men, what spooks love away quickly, how to create an unshakable emotional attachment, and how to reel him in, to name a few.

YOUR TRUE GIRL POWER

As you read this book, understand that it is more the woman than the man who holds the power in a love relationship. Women accomplish this by driving men crazy with desire, keeping them emotionally hooked (with her womanliness, sweetness, peacefulness, warmth, charm, maternal wisdom, honesty, spontaneity, elegance, and human ideals), and moving their hearts toward the spiritual fulfillment of true love.

An enlightened woman does not expect a typical man to fully understand the broad spectrum of love. She wisely takes charge of her love life by choosing her mate wisely, controlling the pace and direction of the relationship, harnessing a male's powerful sexual drive, and teaching a man how to enrich his soul by becoming a more loving person.

This is not a book designed for the passive woman who is simply waiting for her Prince Charming to arrive. It is, however, a valuable resource for any woman who still has the dream of true love and is willing to view things in a slightly different way in order to design the love life she deeply desires for herself.

CATCH THE LOVE YOU WANT

The major theme of this book is:

> Men are like fish.
> A good one with character, plenty of
> action, and tons of love to give can
> be caught by someone like you.

In this modern information age, you don't want to be one of the unfortunate people who misses out on love simply because of a lack of basic awareness or perspective about life's most important values.

Remember the timeless wisdom of Robert Browning, the English poet (1812-1889), who wrote, "What's the earth with all its art, verse, and music worth...compared with love, found, gained and kept?"

Even though past relationships may have left you angry, confused, frustrated, or disappointed with men, there is still no intelligent reason to give up on your dream of finding true love. I believe that getting and keeping the man of your dreams is not a complex process. What every woman needs to know about catching a man is simply that the process of capturing the love of a good man is a lot like how an experienced angler catches a big fish.

With the ideas presented in this book, you can take what you have already experienced, create new empowering attitudes, redesign your romantic package, develop refined personal strategies, and work a more effective, fun, and compelling plan for your love life.

All you really need is a fresh start, deeper compassion for yourself, an unstoppable desire to succeed, a healthy dose of your own feminine creativity, an enlightened sense of humor, and the wisdom to seek a little assistance from the other side.

If a fish could talk, this is what he would honestly say about how to catch him and bring him home for keeps.

Men, the fish, are waiting and eager to bite hard on the promise of true love—hook, line, and sinker.

Good luck and happy fishing!

A visitor walked into the temple asking questions and spouting off opinions about Enlightenment.

The Zen Master listened and sat quietly pouring the visitor a cup of hot tea.

To the visitor's total amazement, the Zen Master continued pouring until the cup overflowed and tea spilled all over the table and onto the floor.

The startled visitor asked the Zen Master, "Why are you continuing to fill up my cup after it is already full of tea?"

The Zen Master replied, "I am trying to show you that you are like this tea cup. You are so full of your own preconceived notions that nothing else can go in. I cannot teach you about Enlightenment until you have first emptied out your cup."

The best way to learn to be a fly-fisherman is to go to a river and ask the trout for a few lessons.

Gwen Cooper and Evelyn Haas
Authors of *Wade a Little Deeper, Dear* (1979)

MEN Are Like FISH

IN THE BLEACHERS
By Steve Moore

"I can see swallowing the hook and maybe the line.
But check out the X-ray. This guy's so gullible,
he swallowed the sinker too."

One

The Book

A DIFFERENT ANGLE ON LOVE

And that's what a miracle is:
a parting of the mists, a shift in
perception, a return to love.

Marianne Williamson
Author of *A Return to Love: Reflections on
the Principles of A Course in Miracles* (1992)

Women who are in search of a new romantic relationship often wonder, "How do men judge the women they date?" The answer to that question and many others face us every week on television with the arrival of romance-reality shows.

In the fall of 2002, an estimated 27 million television viewers watched as Aaron Buerge, a 28 year-old banker from Missouri, dropped to one knee and proposed to Helene Eksterowicz, a 27 year-old grade-school psychologist from New Jersey, on *ABC's* final episode of the hit romance-reality series *The Bachelor*.

This proposal on the two-hour finale capped Buerge's two month dating odyssey with 25 would-be partners as a nationwide television audience eagerly looked on. While the romantic set-up was somewhat unrealistic, the emotions of the people involved seemed nonetheless raw and real.

ABC's The Bachelor attracted an especially large audience of young women ages 18 to 34 who curiously wanted to know what goes on inside a man's head when he's accepting or rejecting a prospective woman. Secretly, many of these women wanted to find out for themselves how they can go about attracting a man's attention and winning his love in their own challenging dating environments.

While to some the show was nothing more than two months of hot tubs, dream dates, catfights, and emotional breakdowns, many other interested people saw *The Bachelor* as a classic example of how men and women fall in love.

Critics of *The Bachelor* like to point out how shallow true love is portrayed in this show. However, for single women starting out on their quest for finding a lifelong marriage partner, the initial challenges are real....how to attract the man of her dreams, how to get him to fall in love, and ultimately how to get her man to joyfully commit to marriage.

This is a book about how men and women date and the critical evaluations that they make along the way. My hope is to answer many of the lingering questions that arise from relating popular romance-reality television shows like *ABC's The Bachelor* and *Fox's Joe Millionaire* to our own love lives.

WHO GETS THE LAST ROSE?

The ultimate goal for a female contestant who appears on *ABC's The Bachelor*, is to be the one who receives the last rose.

In real life the goal is very similar...to be the one woman who finally captures the true love of a highly desirable man.

To the surprise of many, the woman who possesses this seemingly magical ability may not necessarily be the:

- most beautiful
- most glamorous
- most confident
- most intelligent
- most colorful
- sexiest
- kindest
- best-qualified mate

It is like I have been trying to catch a fish by swimming around with them. I keep making myself get in the water again. I try different rivers. I change my stroke. But nothing works. Then I find this guide that tells me about fishing poles and bait, and how to cast and what to do when the line gets taut. The depressing part is that you *know* it will work.

Melissa Bank
Author of *The Girls' Guide to Hunting and Fishing* (1999)

Instead, the woman who ends up attracting, capturing, and keeping the attention and heart of the man she wants (the man who creates and contributes consistent, exciting, and lasting happiness) is simply the woman who is the most clever at playing the game of love.

CLEVER WOMEN LAND THE GOOD ONES!

Webster's Dictionary defines "clever" as "mentally bright; having sharp or quick intelligence; able, inventive."

In this book, I will use the word "clever" to describe a smart woman's uncanny ability to combine knowledge, wisdom, creativity, talent, skill, and intuition in order to take advantage of love opportunities where others usually don't.

While these clever women are capturing wonderful romances, other less enlightened women have to settle for lesser quality love relationships (not very exciting, intimate, passionate, fulfilling, fun, lasting) or worse yet, none at all.

But luckily for you, cleverness is not reserved for the privileged few. In this book, I will show you how cleverness is a learned skill that gets better with intentional study, keen observation, honest feedback, and refined practice.

In this book I offer you a common sense and fundamentally sound thinking model for romantic love. It is designed to reveal fresh ideas that will dramatically enhance your understanding and appreciation of men which in turn will help you to receive back the love that you so deeply cherish.

BASE YOUR DECISIONS ON TIMELESS WISDOM

A smart woman should always be on guard against bad relationship advice, especially from men. What I've done to create more safety for you is build from a base of timeless wisdom. The framework of this book is like the structure of a tree, starting from the roots up. Here's what I mean:

The Roots. An American proverb reads: "A man chases a woman until she catches him." This statement serves as the philosophical support of this book. Without the wisdom of this age-old cultural proverb, this book would be based on nothing more than an unfounded opinion.

The Tree Trunk. A simple and effective way for me to convey my message is through the use of the animated metaphor, "Men are like fish." With the aid of this powerful thinking tool, all a woman has to do conceptually is learn how to catch a man as an experienced angler would catch a big fish.

The Branches. Three main steps in the relationship process include attracting, getting, and keeping the love you want. In fishing terms: attracting is like the bait, getting is like the hook, and keeping is like the net. Other references to angling such as the fishing line, the big fish, fishing holes, crowds, nibbles, and the strike, form the remaining chapters.

The Leaves. Other features that fill out this book include well-researched personal development advice, popular cartoon strips, wise international proverbs, and witty quotations from writers, philosophers, and experts throughout the ages in the areas of love and life. I've sifted through piles of good examples to find the few that I consider most valuable to you.

By following this method, you gain the full benefit of excellent relationship, communication, and personal development advice that stems from a sound philosophical base.

A Shift In Perception Will Change Your Love Life!

The main purpose of this book is to entertain and educate. I also hope to inspire you to take a refreshing new look at your love life by removing its mysteries and easing your fears and limiting self-doubts.

No book can be expected to be the total answer to something as complex as romantic love. But with a little guidance and a new shift in your perception about how relationships work, you can explore your own love life with the renewed enthusiasm of an enlightened adventurer.

> "Adventure can be an end in itself. Self-discovery
> is the secret ingredient that fuels daring."
> Grace Lichtenstein
> Author of *Machisma* (1981)

An ancient Chinese proverb wisely reads, "A journey of a thousand miles begins with the first step."

Congratulations! By reading this brief introductory chapter, you've essentially taken that first step on your new journey to love. All that is required of you from here on out is to stay focused on your outcome (to become a totally loving person and thereby attract into your life the people and circumstances that make love happen), make smarter decisions, and fully enjoy the "fishing for love" process.

The Bottom Line

Don't explore anything or go anywhere without buying yourself a good guidebook and detailed map. You especially don't want to lose your way on the often confusing, ever challenging, and never-ending journey to true love.

A man is like a cat;
chase him and he will run.
Sit still and ignore him
and he'll come purring at
your feet.

Helen Rowland
Author of *A Guide to Men* (1922)

Two

The Proverb

A MAN CHASES A WOMAN UNTIL SHE CATCHES HIM

Behold the proverbs of a people.

Carl Sandburg
American author and poet (1878-1967)

One of the most common complaints that I hear from women about the theme of my book is, "Why is it that us women have to be the ones who do all the work?"

They also say things like, "I'm supposed to be the princess and he's supposed to be my knight in shining armor who sweeps me off my feet. Why hasn't he shown up yet?"

My reply is simply to state the wisdom of this American proverb: A man chases a woman until she catches him.

Wolfgang Mieder, the acclaimed "World's Top Proverb Expert" (by *Smithsonian Magazine*) wrote, "Proverbs can be defined as concise traditional statements expressing an apparent truth with currency among the folk. Defined more inclusively, proverbs are short, generally known sentences of the folk which contain wisdom, truths and traditional views in a metaphorical, fixed, and memorizable form and which are handed down orally from generation to generation."

> "Proverbs are short sayings made out
> of long experiences."
> Zola Neale Hurston
> Author of *Moses: Man of the Mountain* (1939)

The proverb, "A man chases a woman until she catches him" contains elements of truth that have been passed down through several generations of Americans. What was true in your great-grandmother's day is largely true even today.

In this book, we will let the long experience of others guide us wisely on the straight and narrow path to love.

THE PUZZLING LOVE PARADOX

"A man chases a woman until she catches him" is also an example of a figure of speech called a "paradox." A paradox can be defined as "a seemingly contradictory statement that turns out to be full of truth."

The surprise to many men and women is that our proverb means that the catching is not done by the man (the aggressor) but by the woman instead.

> "A man's desire is for the woman; but the woman's desire is rarely other than for the desire of the man."
>
> Samuel Taylor Coleridge
> English poet (1772-1834)

When the man does the catching, he tends to get restless, starts to wander, and eagerly yearns to take part in the catching process (catch lots of fish or catch bigger fish) again.

For most men, the thrill of romantic love lies in the challenge of the chase. And many men live their entire lives in the pursuit of assorted bigger and grander thrills.

However, when the woman does the catching, a man becomes emotionally hooked and more appreciative of a woman. He is less likely to wander and more likely to voluntarily take himself out of the singles' dating game for good.

THE MAN DOES THE CHASING

Gelett Burgess, American humorist and author of *Why Men Hate Women* (1866-1951), wrote, "Men like to pursue an elusive woman, like a cake of wet soap in a bathtub; even men who hate baths."

There are really no men at
all. There are grown-up
boys, and middle-aged boys,
and elderly boys, and even
sometimes very old boys.
But the essential difference
is simply exterior. Your man
is always a boy.

Mary Roberts Rinehart
Author of *Isn't That Just Like a Man!* (1920)

Women who choose to chase and pursue men run the risk of going against human nature. Five million years of evolution have produced men as active hunters, warriors, conquerors, and more recently, aggressive businessmen, and weekend competitive athletes.

To be the object of a woman's desire rather than being the pursuer of a woman may feel instinctively awkward to the majority of traditional men.

A clever or more enlightened woman understands a man's basic aggressive nature by actively attracting him, while at the same time letting him be the chaser. This woman is keenly aware that if she plays the chasing role, a man is more likely to get spooked and run away in the opposite direction.

THE WOMAN DOES THE CATCHING

Love seems to work better not when the man is in full control, but when the woman has the man deeply entranced by her alluring feminine grace.

> **"A man has only one escape from his old self: to see a different self—in the mirror of some woman's eyes."**
> Clare Boothe Luce
> American journalist (1903-1987)

For example, in his earlier years actor Warren Beatty was known as a legendary Hollywood womanizer. According to the *2001 People Weekly Almanac*, he "broke the hearts of many famous actresses, including Natalie Wood, Leslie Caron, and Joan Collins. Collins even had a wedding dress hanging in a wardrobe for almost a year."

Warren Beatty's restless wandering days finally came to an end when actress Annette Benning captured his elusive heart. In 1991 and at the age of 54, he married Benning and by all accounts, lives a happy, married family life.

Beatty recently said, "For me, the highest level of sexual excitement is in a monogamous relationship."

There seems to be little if any peace of mind for a man until he is the one being caught and not when he is the one who is doing the catching.

Ultimately it is the woman and not the man who has the last word on whether a romantic love relationship is going to happen or not.

SOME THINGS ABOUT LOVE NEVER CHANGE

In addition to being filled with useful ideas, this book is founded on sound life principles.

In regards to the value of "sound or correct principles," Stephen R. Covey in his 1989 best-selling book, *The 7 Habits of Highly Effective People*, wrote, "Principles are the territory. Values are the map. When we value correct principles, we have truth—a knowledge of things as they are."

"Principles" can be defined as "time-tested guidelines, rules, laws, practices, or methods for effective operation that are based on wisdom or truth." These principles can be either scientific, mathematical, managerial, financial, psychological, or moral in nature.

A clever or more enlightened woman bases her strategic decisions and plans of actions for finding, attracting, selecting, getting, keeping, improving, and enjoying the love she wants on the following two organizing principles:

The Man Does the Chasing
&
The Woman Does the Catching

For a woman to do otherwise, that is, to chase, pressure, or pursue the man, is more likely to end in failure and frustration than relationship success and happiness.

Even in today's sophisticated world, some things change slowly, if ever at all. This is especially true when it comes to the traditional game of love that is still played between the majority of women and men.

> "Love is like a butterfly which when pursued is just beyond your grasp, but if you will sit down quietly, it may alight upon you."
> Nathaniel Hawthorne
> American writer (1804-1864)

If you want to capture the heart of the man you truly desire, make sure that he feels like he's the one doing the chasing and pursuing. Your romantic challenge is to do a more elegant and subtle job of attracting and persuading.

THE BOTTOM LINE

Every enlightened angler should note that nothing is more important to consistent success in life and love than basing a person's thoughts, beliefs, evaluations, attitudes, decisions, expectations, strategies, skills, and actions on the wisdom of timeless organizing principles.

Three

The Metaphor

MEN ARE LIKE FISH

The greatest thing by far is to be a
master of metaphor. It is the one thing
that cannot be learned from others;
it is also a sign of genius, since
a good metaphor implies
an eye for resemblance.

Aristotle
Ancient Greek philosopher (384-322 B.C.)

Have you ever noticed how people commonly use relationship words and fishing words together? Here are some of the many examples that I noticed in our everyday language: he's a nice catch, she landed a husband, she'd like to hook up with the right guy, there are more fish in the sea, he was the big one that got away, and he's definitely a keeper.

Doesn't this sound a little bit fishy?

In the 1994 hit movie, *Forrest Gump*, the central character played by Oscar-winning actor Tom Hanks said, "Life is a box of chocolates." He wasn't describing life literally. He was merely saying that life was like a box of chocolates (You never know what you're going to get).

"Life is a box of chocolates" is an example of a metaphor.

University professors George Lakoff and Mark Johnson, in their book titled, *Metaphors We Live By*, wrote, "Our ordinary conceptual system, in terms of which we both think and act, is fundamentally metaphorical in nature."

Jonathan Miller, author of *Images and Understanding*, also observed, "Since finding out what something is is largely a matter of discovering what it is like, the most impressive contribution to the growth of intelligibility has been the application of suggestive metaphors."

The word "metaphor" may sound like an esoteric concept, but in reality metaphors are a normal ingredient of our everyday language. They are nothing more than figures of speech that we commonly use to make complex concepts like love easier to understand.

MY TRAINER'S COURSE IN EFFECTIVE METAPHORS

In the summer of 1990, I found myself in a conference room at the Maui Marriott Hotel in Hawaii. I was there to be part of the trainer's team for a two-week personal development seminar hosted by peak performance expert and America's highest-paid motivational speaker Tony Robbins.

During his introductory speech to us seminar trainers, Mr. Robbins said, "I've made a lot more distinctions about global metaphors. You all remember what those are? Yes? No? Global metaphors are symbols that we use to represent large areas of our lives."

> "All perception of truth is the detection of an analogy."
> Henry David Thoreau
> American writer (1817-1862)

The Tony Robbins seminars have taught me how to use effective life metaphors to turn complex concepts into simple ideas. Since that time, I've toyed around with the use of metaphors as a way to understand difficult areas of my life.

One area that needed immediate help was my love life. At the rate I was going, love was going to continue being an irritating source of confusion and frustration.

IGNORANCE ABOUT LOVE IS NOT BLISS

Vernon Howard, author of *Esoteric Mind Power,* wrote, "We are slaves to whatever we don't understand."

The average person may need the equivalent of a bachelor's degree in psychology in order to understand love's complexities. But with the aid of an appropriate metaphor, someone can acquire a good grasp of the subject almost instantly.

As far as our love lives are concerned, ignorance is not bliss. More often than not, ignorance about love inevitably leads to pain, suffering, regret, and disappointment.

On the other hand, knowledge and wisdom are more likely to lead to lasting success and happiness in love and in life.

FINDING AN APPROPRIATE METAPHOR FOR LOVE

On a recent visit to my local bookstore, I stumbled across an interesting little book in the fishing section titled, *Well-Cast Lines: The Fisherman's Quotation Book* by John Merwin.

The back cover of Merwin's book quotes Sir John Buchan (1875-1940), who said, "The charm of fishing is that it is a pursuit of what is elusive but attainable, a perpetual series of occasions for hope."

When you think about it, love has a lot of similarities to fishing. Consider the following:

- **Love can be very elusive.** The harder you chase it, the less likely you seem to get it.

- **Love still seems attainable.** If plenty of average people can have success and happiness in their love lives, why can't the rest of us?

- **Love is a perpetual series of occasions for hope.** Despite our past frustrations and disappointments, we still dream of finding and enjoying true love.

While fishing may not initially conjure up very inspiring images in the minds of many women, the sport of fishing is, nonetheless, rich in mental and metaphorical value.

Pulitzer Prize winning author James Michener praised the sport of fishing when he said, "The high quality of writing devoted to fishing is a tribute to its value."

John Atherton, author of *The Fly and the Fish* (1950), also wrote, "Angling has taught me about art, as art has led to interesting theories and experiments in angling. Thinking and fishing go well together somehow."

In regards to constructing an effective metaphor, fishing and love make an interesting match. Instead of attracting, getting, and keeping the love you want, you'll learn how to entice him to check out your bait, get him emotionally hooked, and land him safely into your net of commitment.

WHAT IS YOUR PROPER ROLE?

As I have alluded to earlier, the next obvious question is this: if love is a lot like fishing, then who should play the role of the angler and who should play the role of the fish?

> "Mark my words, the first woman who fishes
> for him, hooks him."
> William Makepeace Thackeray
> Author of *Vanity Fair* (1847)

A careful examination on the fishing metaphor as it pertains to love leads to an interesting conclusion:

- ❦ The angler as opposed to the fish is the one who prepares for the sport, makes the needed adjustments, and designs an effective strategy of action.

- ❦ In the area of relationships, women buy close to 80 percent of self-help books and watch the majority of "relationship-oriented" television programs.

REEL HIM IN SLOWLY

Be patient. Men fall in love in the spaces; that is, when they are away from a woman and feel her absence. Don't be afraid to let a man go if he wishes to. Every good fisherman knows that pulling too tautly on a line will often snap the rod and pull the fisherman down too. A good woman is one who is secure in her femininity and knows its power. And when she has no power with a particular man, she soon knows that too, and gracefully lets go....Living together, in particular, has been anathema to the contemporary woman's search for commitment. Few women find a long-term living-together arrangement satisfactory....Living with a man is tantamount to overfeeding the fish but never quite getting him on the line. Such fish merely get glutted and bored.

Dr. Toni Grant, Author of *Being a Woman* (1988)
www.drtoni.com

- ◎ The fish is the one who acts on instinct alone in the constant search to satisfy a hunger.

- ◎ Men who allegedly act like a bunch of animals, aren't big buyers of relationship/self-help books and don't represent a large percentage of the viewers who watch or listen to relationship-oriented talk shows. Men are more likely to focus their attention on topics centered around sports, money, cars, computers, business, music, or personal projects.

When it comes to the area of successful love relationships, it bares repeating that the weight of the evidence suggests (to the complete surprise of most men like me) that it is the men who are the fish and it is the women who are the anglers.

CREATE YOUR OWN NEW MENTAL LINKS

Marilyn Ferguson, author of *The Aquarian Conspiracy*, wrote, "Making mental connections is our most crucial learning tool, the essence of human intelligence to forge links; to go beyond the given; to see patterns, relationship, context."

In this case, by making new mental associations between catching a fish and catching a man you will likely expose a wealth of new ideas about love that would never have been thought of before. These gems of thought could only have been created by the cross-linking of the otherwise separate entities of fishing and love.

While some of the newly created images may be quite humorous, the primary value of an outstanding metaphor lies in its uncanny ability to make abstract concepts like love simpler and more concrete.

7 Love Habits of Highly Elusive Men

"It's not the men in my life that counts,
it's the life in my men."
—Mae West in *I'm No Angel* (1933)

Here's my list of the seven habitual ways that desirable men act like fish when it comes to romantic love relationships with women. Anticipate these natural behaviors and plan your personal strategy around them. Remember that you only get one chance at the elusive "Big Fish."

Habit 1: **Highly elusive men love the chase.**
Principle: A man chases a woman until she catches him.
The Bottom Line: Know your role and play it well.

Habit 2: **Highly elusive men seek the most attractive bait first.**
Principle: In the short term, the most talent and game wins.
The Bottom Line: Be outstanding if you can and not poor anywhere.

Habit 3: **Highly elusive men fall off the hook easily.**
Principle: Men have short attention spans and lots of choices.
The Bottom Line: Take up the slack in your small talk.

Habit 4: **Highly elusive men get spooked easily.**
Principle: When a man is cautious or uncertain about you, he's more sensitive to pain than he is to pleasure.
The Bottom Line: Learn how to put a man at ease. Make sure that he doesn't see you at your worst early in the game.

Habit 5: **The big fish are the hardest to catch.**
Principle: Men with major social game savor the challenge.
The Bottom Line: You must create a fear of lost opportunity in order to get him to bite hard now. Also remember that your goal is also to establish an unshakable emotional attachment. That's done by letting him see you at your feminine best when his guard is down.

Habit 6: **Highly elusive men fear the net.**
Principle: A man reserves a last powerful fight for freedom before reaching the state of commitment.
The Bottom Line: Cut him some slack, reel him in slowly, and play him into the net of a more inspiring life with you.

Habit 7: **Highly elusive men will die after being caught.**
Principle: Men understand the desire of the chase. If he feels that the chase is over so is his feeling of love.
The Bottom Line: Don't kill the romance. Keep him chasing. Let him win you over and over again. Remember that it's the chase that feels most real to him. To a typical man desire (emotional intensity) equals love. Until he becomes more enlightened and appreciative about the finer things of love, expect this as normal fish behavior.

Elizabeth Bowen, the Irish-born English novelist and essayist (1899-1973), wrote, "No object is mysterious. The mystery is the eye."

Do yourself a big favor by letting the "men are like fish" metaphor open your eyes and take away some of the mystery. The subject of love, which used to be a complex concept, is now much easier to understand and appreciate.

On a final note, always keep in mind that the answers that most people are searching for in their love lives do not lie in discovering new romantic techniques or accumulating more relationship advice. In nearly all cases, what separates the winners from the losers in love and life is the emotional certainty to take continuous outstanding action that was ultimately created by clear, fundamentally-sound thinking.

THE BOTTOM LINE

"Men are like fish" is a simple metaphor for understanding what it takes to capture the heart of the one you want. Make sure that you have fun with it. The more that you play with the metaphor, the more value you can squeeze out of it. The fresh and imaginative ideas it triggers may surprise, delight, and, most importantly, empower you.

* Check out "7 Love Habits of Highly Elusive Men" on the opposite page for an overview of how highly desirable men tend to behave like an elusive big fish. Remember that the degree to which you are cherished by a man is directly proportionate to how well you understand and appreciate him.

BALLARD STREET   Jerry Van Amerongen

Occasionally, you tie into a big one.

Four

Fishing Lessons

IMPROVE YOUR CHANCES
WITH PREPARATION

For the uninitiated, catching fish is a
simple business: bait a hook, drop it in
the water, see what happens. The
seasoned angler knows better. Fish are
not caught as they are outsmarted.

Criswell Freeman
Author of *The Fisherman's Guide to Life* (1996)

fish•ing les•sons: 1. instructions on how to catch more fish. 2. preparations for attracting, getting, and keeping the love you want. 3. the path chosen by all enlightened anglers.

Top-rated television talk show host Oprah Winfrey (Emmy Award for Best Host of a Talk Show, *The Oprah Winfrey Show*, 1986, 1990, 1991, 1992, 1993, 1994, 1997) said, "Luck is a matter of preparation meeting opportunity."

> "One can present people with opportunities.
> One cannot make them equal to them."
> Rosamond Lehmann
> Author of *The Ballad and the Source* (1945)

Clever women do not leave their love lives entirely to chance. Instead, they understand that preparation and not luck is the true secret to consistent success at attracting, selecting, getting, and keeping the love they want. Examples of love preparation include such things as:

- ✆ Improving your attitude about love
- ✆ Enhancing your physical appearance
- ✆ Refining your communication skills
- ✆ Developing more self-confidence
- ✆ Researching good social opportunities
- ✆ Removing emotional baggage from the past
- ✆ Associating with a better crowd
- ✆ Seeking sound relationship advice

There is no denying that luck does play a critical role in meeting the love you want. But preparation is a far greater factor when it comes to getting, keeping, developing, and maintaining love over the full course of a relationship.

Not to think so would be naive.

A SIMPLE FISHING ANALOGY

A typical question to ask an angler at the end of a busy day of fishing is, "How was your luck?"

In the sport of fishing, luck is definitely a factor. But the expert angler knows that it is important to separate luck from its far more dominant counterpart, skill.

For example, in *The Complete Idiot's Guide to Fishing Basics*, fishing expert Mike Toth writes, "Only 10 percent of fishermen catch 90 percent of the fish. Many fishermen hit the water with hopes that they'll catch fish, but either they don't consider it a serious pursuit or they don't know enough about the sport itself. The vast majority of these types of fishermen go home empty-handed."

> "Luck enters into every contingency. You are a fool if you forget it — and a greater fool if you count upon it."
> Phyllis Bottome
> English-born writer (1884-1963)

Today, smart anglers can improve their chances for success by hiring an expert fishing guide to teach them how to cast their fishing line, set the hook, and land a fish. Anglers can also learn how to read the water for opportunities and what kinds of bait, lures, or flies to use, and when to use them.

In the sport of fishing and in your love life, the typical angler who depends exclusively on luck usually goes home empty-handed. But enlightened anglers who take the extra time and effort to study and master the sport have a far better chance for lasting success.

Don't You Dare Miss Out On Love!

Not catching any fish may be disappointing to an angler, but not experiencing love is far more serious and tragic.

Danish philosopher and theologian, Soren Kierkegaard (1813-1855), warned, "To cheat oneself out of love is the most terrible deception; it is eternal loss for which there is no reparation either in time or in eternity."

> "When you've missed love, you've missed the essence of life."
>
> Dr. Leo Buscaglia
> Author of *Loving Each Other* (1984)

Jim Rohn, modern-day business philosopher and author of *Seven Strategies For Wealth and Happiness,* painted a similar picture when he wrote, "It's better to have a love affair in a tent on the beach, than to live in a mansion all by yourself."

Love plays a far too important role in determining the quality of a person's overall happiness to risk missing out on because of a simple lack of preparation.

Prepare For Your Next Love Opportunity

To paraphrase Benjamin Disraeli, the English statesman and author (1804-1895), "The secret of success in life is for a woman to be ready for her opportunity when it comes."

In order to help you get started in this lifelong learning process remember these important points:

- ✸ **Keep an open mind.** Great ideas only take root in the minds of those who are ready and willing to receive them. Prepare for new ideas by first clearing out the garbage of your old thinking. You can't change your life for the better without first changing your thinking for the better.

- ✸ **Expect more out of life.** A Chinese proverb reads, "Raise your sail one foot and you get ten feet of wind." Dare to believe that you deserve better than what your present circumstances show. You rarely get more than you expect. In order to get more out of life, you've got to start expecting to deserve and receive more in your life.

- ✸ **Become a lifelong learner.** Isaac Walton (1593-1683), the father of fly-fishing wrote, "As no man is born an artist, so no man is born an angler." By the same token, no one is born a lover. We all learn about love or fail to learn about love. The lessons of love for all of us are constant and never-ending.

- ✸ **Start immediately.** A Persian proverb reads, "Go and wake up your luck." Don't procrastinate and hope for the day that love magically appears in your life. Be proactive and do your part to make love happen. There are only so many tomorrows.

- ✸ **Try new approaches.** Helen Keller, the American writer and lecturer (1880-1968), wrote, "Life is a daring adventure or nothing. Avoiding danger is no

The Universal Fishing Laws

"Just as there are laws of nature like gravity,
the universal laws of success can predict
outcomes and explain why some people
triumph while others fail."
—Brian Tracy, Author
The Universal Laws of Success and Achievement

Criswell Freeman, author of *The Fisherman's Guide to Life*, wrote, " Only when we approach the water with respect do we gain its fullest measure of enjoyment. The fish aren't always biting, but Mother Nature is always watching. So we'd best behave ourselves." To help you maintain the integrity of the sport, here are the universal fishing laws that will guide you to love:

THE LAW OF DESTINY: Your decisions about what to focus on and what to do or not do will ultimately determine your destiny. While unenlightened women will continue to rely on luck, the wise ones will plant the seeds of good decisions so they can reap the benefits of a great love life later on.

THE LAW OF RECIPROCATION: If a woman wants to feel cherished by a man, then she will need to understand and appreciate him first. If you tend to criticize and complain about a man, then you will have very little chance of being cherished in return. Seek to be more understanding and less judgmental and you will start turning things around in your love life.

THE LAW OF INDIRECT EFFORT: Seek too hard and you shall not find. In order to catch a man, you must be sure that you are not too direct in your approach. Change your focus beyond the idea of catching a man to becoming a more loving, attractive, and charismatic person and you will have a better chance of gaining the side-benefit of acquiring the love of a man.

THE LAW OF AVERAGES: For a given number of attempts, there's a certain ratio of successes. You increase your number of successes by increasing your number of attempts and by getting better at what you do. What that means to the enlightened woman is to succeed at love she must: 1) never give up, 2) master the skills, and 3) improve her perceptions of love.

THE LAW OF OPPOSITE REACTION: Sometimes, your intended actions will create an opposite reaction. For instance, if you want to impress a man, don't be overly impressed by him. If you want a man to show interest in you, mix in a little bit of disinterest. This has the effect of getting him to chase.

THE LAW OF LOVE: To receive the love of others, you must first love yourself. You cannot give the gift of love to another person unless you already possess that gift inside of you. Develop more compassion for your own struggle to succeed and decide to love and accept yourself as you are now.

*The Bottom Line: Respect and obey the universal laws of love and life. That way the natural forces will be with you, not against you.

safer in the long run than exposure." You are wise in your capacity to experience, not in what you have already experienced. Be willing to change your approach in order to change your results. The love and happiness you want may only be a couple of minor adjustments or decisions away.

☞ **Resolve to take full responsibility of your love life.** A Japanese proverb reads, "A firm resolve pierces even a rock." Release everyone, including yourself, from any blame about past relationship failures. The best you can do now is to learn from the past and start taking charge of your future.

☞ **Don't violate the universal laws.** Make sure that you respect and obey the universal laws of love and life so that you are guided naturally toward the love you desire. (For more insight in this area, refer to the opposite page for "The Universal Fishing Laws.")

☞ **Become an enlightened angler.** Develop a deeper love and appreciation for the sport of life with the understanding that what you get in life is not nearly as important as the kind of person you become.

By following these simple guidelines, you will start turning around your misguided love life and head off in the correct direction toward the true love and happiness you want.

PLAY THE PERCENTAGES WISELY

Nineteenth-century American writer and philosopher, Ralph Waldo Emerson (1803-1882), said, "Shallow men believe in luck. Strong men believe in cause and effect."

I find it fascinating that most people plan their vacations with better care than they plan their lives. Perhaps that is because escape is easier than change....The reason why most people face the future with apprehension instead of anticipation is because they do not have it well designed.

Jim Rohn
"America's Foremost Business Philosopher"
www.jimrohn.com

Even though Emerson was probably not referring to love when he wrote those words, applying his observation to the context of love is nonetheless valid.

For those of you who are still not convinced by the thought of love preparation, the alternative path of neglect was best described by famed college basketball coach, John Wooden (the most successful coach in NCAA college basketball history with eleven National Championships at UCLA) when he wrote, "Failure to prepare certainly means preparing to fail."

> "Love will remain a mystery until you commit
> yourself to solving the mystery and learn to
> master the skill of loving."
> Barbara DeAngelis, Ph.D.
> Author of *Making Love All the Time* (1987)

If love is something that you truly want in your life, play the percentages wisely by choosing the safe path of preparation instead of the risky path of luck. Preparation is the only guaranteed way to achieve consistent long-term success and happiness in love and life.

THE BOTTOM LINE

Men are like fish. Small ones (those that you throw back) are easy to catch and require little or no preparation. But the elusive big fish are challenging and can only be caught with specialized knowledge, deep understanding, supportive beliefs, refined communication skills, personalized strategies, unyielding patience, and consistent outstanding actions. Remember that you only get one chance at the big fish. So you must be prepared when opportunity knocks.

Five

Beginner's Luck

RECAPTURE YOUR LOST INNOCENCE

Innocence is a wild trout. But we
humans, being complicated, have to
pursue innocence in complex ways.

Datus Proper
Author of *What the Trout Said* (1996)

be•gin•ner's luck: 1. the initial success that comes to a person who takes up a new sport or game. 2. catching a big trout the first time you go fishing is simply called "beginner's luck." 3. the good fortune that is attracted to a woman with a fresh, optimistic attitude about love, people, and life.

How would you answer the following questions:

- Do you enjoy the company of men?
- Do you like meeting new people?
- How do you feel about the dating process?
- How optimistic are you about falling in love with someone in the not-too-distant future?
- Do you have an abundance of positive energy to contribute to a loving relationship?

What I'm trying to do with these questions is help you assess your attitude. Attitude is simply a measure of your level of optimism. It is one of the most important elements to finding, attracting, getting, and keeping the love you want.

> "Attitude determines your altitude."
> Zig Ziglar
> Author of *See You at the Top* (1977)

According to *Mary Kirby's Guide to Meeting Men*, "Attitude is simply a way of thinking that translates into action. It's what can make an ordinary-looking woman striking and, by the same token, make a flawless beauty an insipid bore."

A Simple Fishing Analogy

In the sport of fishing, there is a common phenomenon regarding new anglers known as "beginner's luck."

Zane Grey, renowned western romance novelist and avid outdoorsman (1875-1939), wrote, "The preposterous luck of the beginner is well-known to all fishermen. It is an inexplicable thing."

What beginning anglers lack in knowledge, experience, and skill they often make up for by having great attitudes.

> "There is no aphrodisiac like innocence."
> Jean Baudrillard
> Author of *The Ecstasy of Communication* (1988)

In fishing and in your love life, tap into the inexplicable magic of "beginner's luck" by recapturing and retaining your lost innocence, along with its refreshing qualities of youth, vitality, openness, cheerfulness, playfulness, and enthusiasm.

My Friday Night Networking Parties

In Southern California where I live, a woman by the name of Mimi Fane puts on a social networking party every month for so-called "successful eligible singles." All you have to do is get on Mimi's mailing list, show up to her events dressed in casual business attire, and pay ten dollars to get in the door.

Mimi does her best to pack the room with an equal amount of men and women. I know of at least two couples who met at one of Mimi's parties and later married. As a result of these kinds of relationships successes, Mimi Fane's parties have acquired a good reputation for meeting quality dating prospects.

The things I particularly like about men are their differentness, their simplicity, their cleverness, their ability to amuse and re-tell life better than it is, their sense of fun, their intelligence, their dependence on women, their boyishness---even childishness---their ability to devote themselves single-mindedly to their interests, their charm, their insecurity, their character and, above all, when they reveal it, their gentleness and vulnerability.

Anna Ford
English contemporary writer
In *Men: Quotations About Men By Women* (1993)

What's strange about these networking parties is that everyone knows you are there to meet someone. There is no time wasted trying to qualify someone to see if they are available for dating. At Mimi Fane's parties, everyone is available, including (on occasion) Mimi!

After years of going to these networking social events, my friends and I have come up with the same conclusion: the best love prospects for men are the attractive women with the least amount of emotional baggage.

> "Enthusiasm is the divine particle in our composition: with it we are great, generous, and true; without it, we are little, false, and mean."
> L. E. Landon
> Author of *Ethel Churchill* (1837)

The lesson to be learned here is: don't scare away prospective men early by inadvertently carrying around a hefty load of negative attitudes toward dating, love, men, and life.

REJUVENATE YOUR ATTITUDE ABOUT LIFE

While you can't turn back the clock, you can certainly create a similar effect by staying young at heart.

With that in mind, here are a few tips for getting and keeping a fresh attitude in your love life:

- **Remember what you love.** When your experience turns into cynicism, you are essentially finished. Don't let past hurts accumulate and sour your attitude towards love and men. Your chances for love and happiness depend heavily on maintaining pleasurable emotional/mental associations.

◎ **Keep it simple.** Psychologist Leo Buscaglia wrote, "Love is very simple; it is we who are complex." Keep your love life simple and your emotions pure. You don't need to know a thousand things to succeed at love. Become a master of the love basics.

◎ **Put your trust back into love.** Dare to believe that all things happen for a reason and a purpose and it serves you on some level. Regardless of past disappointments, put your unwavering faith back into love. Your success and happiness depend on how optimistic you are about love, life, and yourself.

◎ **Surrender your ego.** Sometimes in order for love to work, you have to forget about yourself and get more involved in life. Be willing to let the chips fall where they may. Realize that part of love is out of your immediate control. In order to find love, you have to be willing to let go of the controls.

◎ **Forget parts of your past.** Sometimes it is necessary to turn your attention completely away from the past. Both good and bad memories, too well remembered, can prevent you from enjoying present happiness to its fullest.

◎ **Let love surprise you once again.** Just when you think you have love figured out, something will come along and bring you back to your knees. That's a good thing, however. For some unexplainable reason, part of love will always remain mysterious and magical. Don't try too hard to figure love out. Let love surprise you once again and learn how to enjoy the adventurous ride of life more fully.

If you follow these guidelines, you can rejuvenate your attitude and revitalize your love life. Soon the sparkle in your eyes will return to delight those who are fortunate to be a part of your new approach to life.

YOUR RETURN BACK TO LOVE

Some women may say, "I'm too experienced to be innocent again. When it comes to love, I've been there, done that."

All I can say is take heart in some words of wisdom from American novelist and essayist, James Baldwin (1924-1987), that brought back hope for me: "Experience, which destroys innocence, also leads one back to it."

Stay fascinated in love. Learn all you can, but keep a healthy respect for love's magic. Love has a habit of being wooed by a person's innocence instead of their experience.

> **"Youth is a quality, and if you have it,
> you never lose it."**
> Frank Lloyd Wright
> American architect (1867-1959)

Return to love with the healthy expectation of exciting and challenging things to come and you can tap into the "inexplicable luck of the beginner."

Remember that the heart that loves is forever young.

THE BOTTOM LINE

Beginner's luck comes to those who expect the best. You can change your love life for the better, by first changing your attitude for the better. Outstanding results naturally follow outstanding attitudes.

SINGLE SLICES   by Peter Kohlsaat

Six

The Fish Story

LET GO OF THE BIG ONE THAT GOT AWAY

In every species of fish I've angled for,
it is the ones that have got away that
thrilled me the most, the ones that
keep fresh in my memory. So I say
it is good to lose fish.

Ray Bergman
Author of *Trout* (1949)

fish sto•ry: 1. an implausible, boastful, incredible story owing to the fact that fishermen tend to exaggerate the size of their catch. 2. a lost love affair that you can't easily forget. 3. your underlying excuse for living in the past instead of the present.

Some people are hard to forget, especially the ones who leave you shattered with a broken heart.

English poet laureate, William Wordsworth (1770-1850), wrote, "Though nothing can bring back the hour of splendor in the grass, or glory in the flower; we will grieve not, rather find strength in what lies behind."

While some people may feel that it is a romantic thing to reflect back fondly on past love affairs, it's an entirely different beast when those same memories prevent a person from experiencing present and future happiness to the fullest.

A SIMPLE FISHING ANALOGY

In fishing terminology, a "fish story" is a boastful tale about how the big fish escaped capture. The common occurrence is for the angler to greatly exaggerate the size of the fish that was initially hooked but later managed to get away.

Some interesting observations that can be drawn from the lessons of "fish stories" include:

- Nothing grows faster than a fish from the time he bites until the time he gets away.
- The fish that escaped is the big one.
  (Chinese proverb)

- ✎ A fish is larger for being lost. (Japanese proverb)

- ✎ There is a critical difference between "hooking" a fish and actually "landing" it in the net.

- ✎ All anglers have an escaped fish in their memory that still haunts them.

In the sport of fishing and in your love life, remember that the thrills of the big ones that got away always appear far better in retrospect than they actually were.

A BIG ONE THAT GOT AWAY

Stories of lost love happen to both men and women alike. Here's my personal reference of how deeply painful it can feel from a man's perspective.

A few years ago, I found myself working in a new career as a professional tour director. At the time I was traveling with a motorcoach full of senior citizens from California on an escorted sightseeing trip called, "Autumn in New England with AFC Tours."

> "A long past vividly remembered is like
> a heavy garment that clings to your limbs
> when you would run."
>
> Mary Antin
> Author of *The Promised Land* (1912)

We were driving by beautiful fall foliage along the Mohawk Trail in central Massachusetts. The deepening shadows at that time of year, the rich color of the leaves, and the unique fragrance of autumn in the air reminded me of my trip to see a woman I dearly loved years ago.

Our losses include not only our separations and departures from those we love, but our conscious and unconscious losses of romantic dreams, impossible expectations, illusions of freedom and power, illusions of safety--- and the loss of our younger self, the self that thought it would always be unwrinkled, invulnerable and immortal.

Judith Viorst
Author of *Necessary Losses* (1986)

A passenger in the front row of the motorcoach asks me, "Steve, you seem to know a lot about this area. How many times have you been here to New England?"

I reply, "I've only been here a few times. The first time was to visit a woman that I really liked. We had one of those 'Love Boat' cruise ship romances many years ago."

"Hey, Steve, whatever happened to her?" asks another passenger eavesdropping from a few rows back.

I answer, "She's still around. And everything is just fine between us. There is, however, a slight problem. You see she lives in Connecticut and I live in California. She also happens to be married to a guy named Paul. And she has two young sons. Aside from that, things couldn't be better."

A few of the passengers laughed. Others looked at me with pity. In spite of my joking around and the passing of several years, my sadness of lost love must have still showed.

Although I'll probably never forget the splendor of that wonderful romance, I've been able to move ahead in my love life with the help of a fishing perspective.

LET GO OF THE PAST....FINALLY!

If you have a "fish story" that is getting in your way of present and future happiness, here are some ways to help you complete your unfinished past:

- ℘ **Find a moral to your story.** Close out that seemingly never-ending chapter of your love life by putting an empowering final moral to your fish story. Count your blessings for the experience one last time. Then turn the page and start a new chapter.

- ✆ **Focus on the love life in front of you.** A French proverb reads, "New love drives out old love." Like driving a car, you must quit looking in the rear-view mirror at your romantic past and keep your eyes focused on the new love opportunity that is about to appear in front of you.

- ✆ **Think abundance not scarcity.** An old saying goes, "There are plenty of fish in the sea." Realize that it only takes one fish in the sport of love. If you maximize your social opportunities, there will be plenty of good men for you to choose from.

- ✆ **Take bold steps.** A German proverb reads, "Boldly ventured is half won." If it becomes necessary, get rid of all the old love letters, turn off the sad love songs, and remove other unwanted reminders that keep you glued to a time that will never return.

- ✆ **Outgrow your past.** A lost love from sixth grade shouldn't hurt too much when you graduate from college. That's because you're not the same person when you graduate from college as you were in sixth grade. Use the same principle in your adult life in order to outgrow your past loves.

- ✆ **Never look back.** It's tough to eliminate the past. But if the mere thought of the past brings up consistent regret and loss, then take one last look, freeze that moment in time forever, and then never look back. Ever!

Follow these steps and you will leave the unwanted part of your past where it properly belongs—behind you.

GATHER UNSTOPPABLE FORWARD MOMENTUM

The final and most important step to letting go of the big one that got away is to move decisively ahead in your love life.

Remember these important words of wisdom from Benjamin Disraeli, English prime minister, author, and statesman (1804-1881): "The magic of first love is our ignorance that it can never end."

Make a firm decision and refuse to remain stuck in your love life. Keep moving forward in the direction of pleasurable new love opportunities until you find the right situation.

> "Don't limit yourself to the idea of one life—
> one love. Plan to have at least four important
> loves in your life."
>
> Sally Jessy Raphael
> Author of *Finding Love* (1984)

For love to happen again, you must complete your relationship "fish stories." Let go of the big ones that got away, learn from your mistakes, count your blessings, and turn the page to the present. The compelling new love of your life is now properly in front of you, not behind.

THE BOTTOM LINE

Men are like fish. Once you lose them, they are almost impossible to catch with the same bait again. Learn to discipline your disappointment. Realize that even the most thrilling hook-ups are often lost on the way to the landing net. Play it smart by making the clear-cut decision to move directly ahead toward your next love opportunity.

I know there are nights when I have power, when I could put on something and walk in somewhere, and if there is a man who doesn't look at me, it's because he's gay.

Kathleen Turner, American Actress
from *An Uncommon Scold* by Abby Adams
(1989)

Seven

The Fishing Rod

GET A FIRM GRIP
ON YOUR SELF-CONFIDENCE

Confidence—the single most
important item an angler needs.
Without this essential requirement,
many fish otherwise taken,
will be lost.

Peter Lightfoot and Kevin Whay
Authors of *Stillwater Trout Fly-Fishers' Ready Reference*
from *The Angler's Quotation Book* by Eric Restall

fish•ing rod: 1. a long, slender pole made out of wood, steel, or fiberglass for use with a reel in catching fish. 2. the main piece of equipment in fishing. 3. a woman's self-confidence.

Samuel Johnson, the 18th century English author, wrote, "Self-confidence is the first requisite to great undertakings."

All the knowledge and talent in the world is of little value without following through by taking outstanding actions. And nothing takes away from the quality of a person's actions more than an overabundance of fear and self-doubt.

> "You've got to take the initiative and play your game. In a decisive set, confidence is the difference."
>
> Chris Evert
> Tennis world champion

Before you start expanding your knowledge and improving your skills for attracting, getting, and keeping love, make sure you solidify your base of self-confidence.

A SIMPLE FISHING ANALOGY

A visit to the fishing department of a sporting goods store will put you in front of all sorts of angling equipment. You will find a variety of items such as bait, lines, hooks, sinkers, flies, fishing rods, tackle boxes, fishing reels, landing nets, and trolling lures. From this selection, the first item that a novice should buy is a fishing rod.

According to *Fishing For Dummies* by Peter Kaminsky, "The

rod is the symbol of the angler in the same way that a gun is the symbol of the hunter. Just as you need a bullet or shell to shoot an animal, you need a reel and a line to catch a fish. But the rod, like the gun, is the main ingredient."

In the sport of fishing and in your love life, it is critical to determine what is the main ingredient to your success and start building from there.

CONFIDENCE IS SOMETHING YOU CAN LEARN

A few years ago, I went to the Club Med Village at Sonora Bay, Mexico. One of the people vacationing there was a fascinating young woman from San Francisco named Angela.

All the men (and women) at Club Med couldn't help but notice Angela. Besides being stunningly attractive, she also radiated an air of absolute self-confidence.

> "Sex appeal is 50% what you've got and 50% what people think you've got."
> Sophia Loren
> Italian-born actress

One afternoon on the water-ski dock, I got a chance to talk with Angela. I discovered that she was a professional model. She said that her training for modeling included learning how to dress, how to groom, how to walk, how to pose, and how to handle herself in a variety of social situations with poise and elegance (For example: how to reject a guy like me without creating excessive emotional damage).

Angela's confidence training paid off big the following year, when I opened up a *Playboy Magazine* and saw her as the Centerfold Playmate of the Month.

To have "It," the fortunate possessor must have that strange magnetism which attracts both sexes. He or she must be entirely unself-conscious and full of self-confidence, indifferent to the effect he or she is producing, and uninfluenced by others. There must be physical attraction, but beauty is unnecessary.

Elinor Glyn
Author of *The Man and the Moment* (1915)

GET A FIRM GRIP ON YOUR SELF-CONFIDENCE

To help you raise your level of self-confidence, here are some valuable pointers worth mentioning:

- ℗ **Start by being kind to yourself.** A Yiddish proverb reads, "Do not make yourself low; people will tread on your head." Be your own best supporter instead of the leading critic. Listen carefully to how you talk to yourself. If you don't like what you hear, change it immediately. You can't rise to the top in life if you're constantly tearing yourself down.

- ℗ **Stop comparing yourself with others.** Doubt usually comes from comparing yourself with others who are superior to you in some narrow context. Realize that all people have both strengths and weaknesses. Refuse to play the no-win comparison game. You'll either destroy yourself or destroy others along the way. Neither are good for your psyche.

- ℗ **Build from your strengths.** You can't be masterful at everything, but there are a few areas that you can be really good at. Find your areas of strength and build your confidence around these. Handle your weaknesses but move ahead in life with your strengths.

- ℗ **See the big picture more clearly.** Confidence at love comes from knowing things that others don't. By adopting this model, you'll know what the pieces are to the love puzzle and how they fit together to give you a clear picture of your love life. Instead of being confused and surprised by men, you'll anticipate more opportunities and gain better results.

⚉ **Generate an internal source of pride**. Another powerful way to build your self-esteem is by creating new personal breakthroughs. These become memorable examples where you have demonstrated the ability to overcome obstacles and succeed.

⚉ **Take good care of your own emotional needs.** Ease the pressure off of your future romantic relationships by making sure that you continuously nurture your own security, variety, connection, recognition, growth, and contribution needs beforehand.

⚉ **Get in excellent physical shape.** A healthy diet, vigorous exercise, proper hydration, and plenty of rest can do wonders for strengthening your mind, body, and spirit. You can't rise to meet your challenges in life if your body is constantly letting you down.

⚉ **Cultivate boldness.** A French proverb reads, "The bashful always lose." Take smart chances and live your life with no regrets. There is nothing to lose in your love life except lost opportunities. Be bold and take decisive intelligent actions more often.

⚉ **Shift your focus toward self-actualization.** Set your sights higher by striving to become all of the great things that you can possibly be. Your journey toward a more compelling future will naturally yield the desired by-products of enhanced self-esteem and increased self-confidence.

When you possess unshakable confidence in yourself, you enjoy the freedom to go into any situation and perform with effectiveness, playfulness, flexibility, and peace of mind.

BEGIN BY LOVING YOURSELF FIRST

While you are going through this challenging confidence building process, remember the helpful advice of actress-comedian Lucille (*I Love Lucy*) Ball, who said, "I have an everyday religion that works for me. Love yourself first and everything else falls into line. You really have to love yourself to get anything done in this world."

> "Beneath the surface of our daily life, in the personal history of many of us, there runs a continuous controversy between an Ego that affirms and an Ego that denies."
>
> Beatrice Webb
> Author of *My Apprenticeship* (1926)

Self-confidence is really nothing more than trusting and accepting yourself. For many people this may be a slow building process. But for others, confidence begins the instant they decide to have more compassion for their own human struggle and to simply love themselves unconditionally.

For others to love you, you must first love yourself.

THE BOTTOM LINE

The quality of your actions are either increased or decreased by how you feel about yourself. Start your new love life by getting a firm grip on your self-confidence. It is the main ingredient to your success and happiness at love.

* Go to page 193 for acquiring the additional perspective of "Uncanny Advice for Fish (Men)." Appreciate the lessons that all men need to know in order to be caught by true love.

Quality Time

by Gail Machlis

Eight

The Bait

Make your attraction more powerful

You cannot bring a hook into a fish's
mouth unless there is food on it
that pleases him.

Dame Juliana Berners
Author of *Treatise of Fishing with an Angle* (1450)
from
Well-Cast Lines by John Merwin

bait: 1. a piece of food that is used to entice or lure a fish. 2. the presentation of alluring feminine qualities that powerfully attract men. 3. the first skill of romantic love.

An American proverb reads, "A man chases a woman until she catches him." What that means to a woman is: if a man doesn't chase you, then there is no chance of catching him.

The force that causes a man to chase is something called "attraction." Attraction works like a magnet. The more powerful the magnet, the more it will attract.

Jim Rohn, modern-day business philosopher and author of *Seven Strategies For Wealth and Happiness,* wrote, "To attract attractive people, you first must be attractive. Go to work on yourself. If you become attractive, you can attract."

If you want a wide range of quality men to choose from, then you'd better make your attraction as powerful as you possibly can.

A SIMPLE FISHING ANALOGY

In the sport of fishing, bait is used to attract a fish to the angler's fishing line.

My personal favorite choice for catching trout is a product called *Power Bait.* The label on the outside of the jar reads, "Fish Bite and Won't Let Go! *Berkeley Power Bait* contains advanced scent and flavor that dispenses to attract trout, salmon, and steelhead. Firmly cover the hook with floating Trout Bait for best results."

yourself into the best possible package for today. There's nothing worse than having to watch a tired, outdated act. Keep your bait fresh and stay current with your love life of today.

⑨ **Maximize your physical talents.** Do all you can in terms of improving and refining your beauty, attire, health, fitness, vitality, voice quality, and physical movements. The woman who looks outstanding, sounds alluring, touches with warmth, and is stunning to watch in action gets the initial and consistent attention of men.

⑨ **Develop your game.** The key element of attraction that brings a man's passion to a boil is when a woman has the confidence and ability to play the game of love well. Find ways to increase your ability to communicate, entertain, and persuade effectively. Smart women know that it is far more important to move men emotionally, than it is intellectually. The woman with the most "wiggle" in her social game creates the greatest ongoing intrigue.

⑨ **Play with more heart.** A Philippine proverb reads, "Beauty will fade, but not goodness." Demonstrate your positive emotional range in terms of the qualities of warmth, compassion, gratitude, joy, desire, sincerity, tolerance, understanding, sensitivity, generosity, and flexibility. Beware of deductions that are made against you for negative displays of anger, criticism, jealousy, bitterness, sarcasm, or cynicism. Quality men will do their most crucial measuring around the heart of a woman.

The Bait Self-Quiz

HOW POWERFULLY DO YOU ATTRACT MEN?

Check your bait. (Circle your choices & add up the score.)

TALENT: HOW PHYSICALLY APPEALING ARE YOU TO MEN?

• Physical appearance	Poor	Fair	Good	Excellent
• Womanliness/femininity	Poor	Fair	Good	Excellent
• Voice qualities	Poor	Fair	Good	Excellent
• Fitness/vitality/wellness	Poor	Fair	Good	Excellent

GAME: HOW WELL DO YOU CAPTIVATE MEN'S ATTENTION?

• Sexual intrigue	Poor	Fair	Good	Excellent
• Confidence/elegance	Poor	Fair	Good	Excellent
• Conversational charm	Poor	Fair	Good	Excellent
• Common sense	Poor	Fair	Good	Excellent

HEART: HOW WELL DO YOU MOVE HIS EMOTIONS?

• Emotional warmth & kindness	Poor	Fair	Good	Excellent
• Ability to listen & understand	Poor	Fair	Good	Excellent
• Sense of gratitude & appreciation	Poor	Fair	Good	Excellent
• Ability to laugh & enjoy	Poor	Fair	Good	Excellent

CLASS: HOW MUCH RESPECT DO YOU COMMAND?

• Sense of responsibility	Poor	Fair	Good	Excellent
• Ability to handle adversity	Poor	Fair	Good	Excellent
• Honesty & integrity	Poor	Fair	Good	Excellent
• Basic financial stability	Poor	Fair	Good	Excellent

Points:
Excellent	4
Good	3
Fair	2
Poor	0

Total Score:
53-64	Simply irresistible
40-52	Worth a good look
26-39	One in the crowd
0-25	Won't get a nibble

THE BOTTOM LINE:

You can only catch the ones who chase your bait. The most attractive bait always receives the first serious look.

☞ **Move up in class.** In the sport of horse racing, the winner is often not the fastest horse but the one with the most class. Class determines how much strength remains for the critical challenge of the final stretch. Go to work on refining your elements of poise, elegance, command, taste, grace, charm, and style. These qualities will stand out when the going gets tough and push you ahead of the pack.

It doesn't take a thousand minor things to be successful in any phase of life. It only takes the mastery of the basics.

FIND A PERSONAL LOVE COACH

Ann Landers, nationally-syndicated columnist and relationship author, advised, "Don't accept your dog's admiration as conclusive evidence that you are wonderful."

> **"Women look for talent, men for beauty."**
> Vietnamese proverb

Attraction is a major part of the love game. In order to play the game to win, be sure to find yourself a good coach or confidant who has your best interests in mind.

When the competition gets tough, intelligent people seek out high-quality advice and accurate honest feedback. That's true in sports, business, life, and love.

One piece of important advice in a critical area of your love life may be all you need to succeed. It could be something like remedying bad breath, changing your hair style, getting in better physical shape, interacting with more confidence, speaking in more pleasant sounding tones, becoming

Advice for a teenage daughter—five inexpensive beauty hints:

For attractive lips, speak words of kindness.

For lovely eyes, seek out the good in people.

For a slim figure, share your food with the hungry.

For beautiful hair, let a child run his fingers through it once a day.

And for poise, walk with the knowledge that you will never walk alone.

Sam Levenson
American humorist and author (1911-1980)

a friendlier person, learning how to be a better listener, being more approachable, going to new places, associating with a better crowd, dating men who are better suited for you, or becoming less judgmental and more tolerant.

Find someone you can trust and ask them for help. At first, be sure to brace yourself for the feedback. Then brainstorm with supportive friends for workable solutions, make the necessary adjustments, and eventually reap the benefits.

> "Advice is what we ask for when we already
> know the answer but wish we didn't."
> Erica Jong
> Author of *How to Save Your Own Life* (1977)

Remember that the greatest number of love choices usually go to the women who possess the most powerful ability to attract men.

Before you go looking for love, make sure your bait is absolutely irresistible. Otherwise, you may have to settle for less choice or lower quality than you potentially deserve.

THE BOTTOM LINE

Men are like fish. You can only catch the ones who chase after your bait. The most attractive and available bait always receives the first serious look.

* Gauge how powerfully you attract men by taking "The Bait Self-Quiz" back on page 80. Then go to page 194 for "Notes on the Bait Self-Quiz." Discover whether you presently qualify as being simply irresistible, worth a good look, one in the crowd, or if you won't even get a nibble.

SINGLE SLICES by Peter Kohlsaat

Nine

The Fishing Line

TAKE UP THE SLACK IN YOUR SMALL TALK

If there is a lot of slack line, the fish will
be able to shake his head to throw out
the hook. Slack line will almost
always cause trouble.

Cathy Beck
Author of *Cathy Beck's Fly-Fishing Handbook* (1996)

fish•ing line: 1. a string, usually made out of monofilament plastic, that is used to catch fish. 2. the connection or bond between the angler and the hooking device. 3. small talk or casual conversation.

What you say and how you say it can either help or hurt your chances for love.

Oscar Wilde, Irish playwright and wit (1854-1900), said, "Ultimately, the bond of all companionship, whether marriage or friendship, is conversation."

> "Each person's life is lived as a series of conversations."
>
> Deborah Tannen
> Author of *You Just Don't Understand* (1990)

If you want to maintain a strong bond or connection with a prospective romance, be sure you acquire and maintain excellent conversational skills.

A SIMPLE FISHING ANALOGY

In the sport of fishing, the fishing line is what connects the angler with the fish. When a fish falls off the hook, it is often the result of too much slack in the line.

Slack line is the result of carelessness and neglect.

In order to prevent this unfortunate event from happening, maintain a tight responsive connection with your catch by taking up all the unnecessary slack in your line.

That applies to both fishing and your love life.

MY SINGLES' DINING & DATING CLUB

A few years ago in the hope of increasing the number of quality choices in my social life, I bought a membership in a singles' dining club called "*A Table For Six*." For an additional cost of fifteen dollars plus the price of dinner, I got the opportunity to leisurely dine at a nice local restaurant with three single women and two other single men.

One of the most obvious things that stood out in this social situation was how well or how poorly people were at casual conversation or small talk.

> "Conversation is like a dear little baby that is brought in to be handed round. You must rock it, nurse it, keep it on the move if you want it to keep smiling."
>
> Katherine Mansfield
> Author of *The Doves' Nest* (1923)

For example, some friendly discussions escalated into heated debates. Other times conversations veered off into sensitive subjects like religion, abortion, politics, sex, and money. And still other conversations were simply boring.

"*A Table For Six*" was like a conversational appetizer. If you liked the taste of the appetizer, then you were likely to dig into more of the same.

But as many of us in the dating club discovered, after one dining experience with a poor conversationalist we had more than our fill of that person.

IMPROVE YOUR COMMUNICATION SKILLS

The quality of your relationship with another person is no

The conversation of two people remembering, if the memory is enjoyable to both, rocks on like music or lovemaking. There is a rhythm and a predictability to it that each anticipates and relishes.

Jessamyn West
Author of *The State of Stony Lonesome* (1984)

better than the quality of your communications both in talking and in listening. Unfortunately few people ever take the time to examine how well they converse.

Oliver Wendell Holmes, American novelist and essayist (1809-1894), pointed out, "Talking is one of the fine arts, the noblest, the most important, and the most difficult."

For improved communications, here are a few valuable pointers that will serve you well in taking up large amounts of slack in your small talk:

- ⑨ **Be brief.** Mark Twain (Samuel L. Clemens) wrote, "The worst kind of death is to be talked to death." Don't bore people with long monologues. Learn to say what you have to say quickly, get to the point, and let the other person have a chance to speak.

- ⑨ **Watch your audience closely.** Keep your audience awake and involved in your small talk. Also learn to distinguish between courtesy and genuine interest. If your audience starts to fidget, it probably means that they are not really listening to you. That's your cue to stop talking and start listening.

- ⑨ **Have something good to say.** Find ways to increase your range of interesting topics by either study or experience. Learn to broaden your horizons day-to-day and week-to-week so you will have something of value to talk about. Stay current by reading a high quality daily newspaper like the *USA Today*.

- ⑨ **Learn the art of saying it well.** Become more adept at the regular use of humor, sincerity, candor, and enthusiasm. Learn to tell a story that is fresh, colorful, enjoyable, and alive. Talking has a lot more to do with how well you express things rather than the content of what you actually say. An outstanding conversationalist can make even mundane topics sound extraordinary.

⊕ **Learn what not to say.** Dorothy Neville, author of *Under Five Reigns* (1910), wrote, "The real art of conversation is not only to say the right thing in the right place, but, far more difficult still, to leave unsaid the wrong thing at the tempting moment." Sometimes in our quest for lively conversation we have to choose between what is honest, what is advantageous, and what is better off being left unsaid. Each option has its appropriate moment.

⊕ **Back your words with emotion.** Be sure to reinforce your small talk with the power of your emotions. People are more impressed and moved by how you feel than by what you know. Express with appropriate emotion and you can impress with impact.

⊕ **Adjust your voice control dials.** Research in human communications shows that the tone of your voice conveys more meaning than the words you actually use. Carefully adjust your volume, pitch, speed, rhythm, and voice textures for the enjoyment of the listener. A pleasant sounding voice gives a tremendous unconscious boost to any woman's appeal.

A German proverb reads, "Practice makes the master." No matter where you are in terms of your present skill level, you will become increasingly effective at communicating and interacting with others by practicing with the clear purpose of becoming a conversational master.

JUDGE BY THE RESPONSE YOU GET

The final point to remember is that the quality of your communications is not determined by how eloquent you think you sound. Instead the quality of your communication skills is wisely judged by the quality of the response you get.

Samuel Johnson, English author and lexicographer (1709-1784), observed, "The happiest conversation is that of which nothing is distinctly remembered but a general effect of pleasing impression."

The best-crafted speech and the noblest of intents are of little value if your target audience reacts in a negative way.

> "Too much brilliance has its disadvantages,
> and misplaced wit may raise a laugh, but
> often beheads a topic of profound interest."
> Margot Asquith
> Author of *More or Less About Myself* (1934)

Overall, it is the woman who keeps a man fascinated and hungry for more connection that has done an outstanding job of taking up the slack in her line.

THE BOTTOM LINE

Men are like fish. Remember to take up the slack in your small talk so that you maintain a good connection with your prospective catch. Otherwise, an elusive man will fall off the emotional hook because of declining interest.

i need help

Ten

The Hook

USE ONLY THE MOST SECURE DEVICES

People become emotionally "hooked"
on those persons who can truly satisfy
their never-ending need
for human understanding.

Thomas McKnight and Robert Phillips
Authors of *Love Tactics: How to Win the Love You Want*
(1988)

hook: 1. a curved or sharply bent piece of metal used to catch fish. 2. a capturing device that is disguised or covered with bait. 3. the key elements that secure a man to a woman.

A romantic relationship is in trouble the minute a man starts losing interest in a woman. With this awareness, a clever woman makes sure that her man's attention is firmly secured. There are two ways to accomplish this. One way is by tricking a man with deception and manipulation. The other way is by filling a man's deepest emotional needs, quickly and elegantly.

Both of these methods can work very well in the short term. But the latter method is the more dependable, lasting, ethical, and enlightened approach.

If you want to secure your love for the long-term, stick with consistently filling a man's deepest emotional needs.

A SIMPLE FISHING ANALOGY

In the sport of fishing, the device that keeps the fish on the line is called a hook or fishhook.

Last fall, I took a trip to Springfield, Missouri to visit the largest sporting goods store in America called *The Bass Pro Shop*. While I was there, I discovered that fishhooks come in various shapes, sizes, and qualities. Fishhooks can be barbed, treble, snelled, long shank, open bend, clawbeak, weedless, and salmon egg hooks, to name a few.

A Japanese company now makes a hot-selling brand of fishhooks that are seven times sharper and four times stronger than average ones. These high-quality hooks help prevent fish from falling off and escaping during the difficult landing process.

Gene Kugach, author of *Fishing Basics: The Complete Illustrated Guide*, wrote, "The most important thing to remember when buying hooks is to look for hooks made by a reputable manufacturer. Cheap hooks lose fish."

For consistent success in fishing and in your love life, use only the highest quality and most secure hooking devices.

THE HIGHEST QUALITY LOVE HOOK

There is no denying that outstanding beauty is one of the most obvious ways to "hook" a man.

But beauty alone does not secure love over the long-term. Otherwise, the rate of failed love relationships would not be so high historically among Hollywood celebrities.

> "Love built on beauty, soon as beauty, dies."
> John Donne
> English poet & clergyman (1572-1631)

William James, American psychologist and philosopher (1842-1910), suggested that rather than desire for beauty, "The deepest principle in human nature is their craving to be appreciated."

By learning the art of sincere appreciation, a person can better secure a lasting relationship. Three sensitive areas to look at when you appreciate a man include:

- **Respect.** Appreciate a man for his knowledge, expertise, power, accomplishments, or prestige.

They used to say that the fastest way to a man's heart was through his stomach. Now we know better. The fastest and surest way to a man's heart is through his ego. This is the most sensitive part of a man, the part that responds most enthusiastically to a woman's interest.

Mary Kirby
Author of *Mary Kirby's Guide to Men* (1983)

Men who pride themselves on their achievements respond especially well to acts of recognition.

- @ **Like.** Appreciate a man for his sense of humor, wit, personality, and personal charm. Most men (as well as women) respond well to being liked by others.

- @ **Attractiveness.** Appreciate a man for his physical appearance, fitness, strength, and taste in attire. Men like to be physically appealing to women.

Men and women alike respond well to sincere appreciation. It is a basic principle in human nature.

ENHANCE YOUR LISTENING SKILLS

Dr. Joyce Brothers, psychologist and nationally-syndicated columnist, wrote, "Listening, not imitation, may be the sincerest form of flattery.... If you want to influence someone, listen to what he says."

> "Men aren't attracted to me by my mind.
> They're attracted by what I don't mind."
> Gypsy Rose Lee
> American actress & burlesque entertainer (1914-1970)

Listening is the most basic form of sincere appreciation. Here are a few simple suggestions for making your listening more effective:

- @ **Show sincere interest.** Find something that is (or could be if you really wanted to) fascinating, enjoyable, agreeable, or interesting in what a man has to say. A man is often impressed more by what a woman listens to rather than what she says.

⑨ **Ask a thought-provoking question.** Search for deeper meaning or clarification by asking a thought-provoking question. If you can, ask questions that elicit resourceful feelings like pride, excitement, enjoyment, passion, or love that empower the man.

⑨ **Give a highly-valued compliment.** Find something positive about a subtle character trait or the good tastes of a man in regards to his possessions. Men are especially disarmed by a timely and sincere person-centered compliment.

⑨ **Pause before replying.** Give extra value to what a man has to say by pausing briefly before replying. Pausing before responding is a classy act. It demonstrates subtle, yet powerful respect for what a man has to say.

⑨ **Reinforce with candor.** Never underestimate the power of candor. You can score a direct hit to the heart of a man by using the bold honesty of properly measured straight talk when the appropriate moment arises.

⑨ **Perceive rather than judge.** Form the additional habit of seeing things from the man's point of view. Getting perturbed about what a man says only shuts off his willingness to be open to you in the future. At the same time, he may also shut off his heart to you for good.

Practice and perfect your listening skills and you will show sincere appreciation in the most subtle yet powerful way.

CREATE AN UNSHAKABLE ATTACHMENT

A woman's goal is to persuade the man she is interested in that he is deeply appreciated in the present and in the foreseeable future.

The degree to which a woman can consistently, creatively, and elegantly appreciate a man in the most sensitive areas of his life will determine the quality and strength of her emotional, physical, and spiritual connection.

> "What do we call love, hate, charity, revenge,
> humanity, magnanimity, forgiveness? Different
> results on the one Master Impulse: The necessity
> of securing one's self-approval."
> Mark Twain
> American writer (1835-1910)

If you use the highest quality hooks, you can withstand the inevitable cross-currents of adversity (emotional upsets, bad news, the negative influence of others, conflicting/changing priorities, growing pains, etc.) that eventually hit all love relationships over time.

Cheap hooks lose fish.

Only quality hooks can keep your love secure.

THE BOTTOM LINE

Men are like fish. The big ones put up a good fight in order to avoid being caught. Use only the highest quality hooks to insure that the love you want doesn't escape. Remember that all smart anglers concentrate their efforts on achieving and maintaining an unshakable (physical, emotional, and spiritual) attachment.

Quality Time
by Gail Machlis

Handsome male, loyal, attentive, fun-loving, offers unconditional love. I'm easy, I don't smoke, drink or do drugs. Love food, long walks on the beach...

NET DATE

machlis 7/21 Finally, Mr. Right

www.uexpress.com

©1998 Gail Machlis/Dist. by Universal Press Syndicate

Eleven

The Big Fish

DECIDE EXACTLY WHAT YOU WANT TO CATCH

The fish is not so much your quarry
as your partner.

Arnold Gingrich
Author of *The Well-Tempered Angler* (1965)

big fish: 1. what every angler dreams of catching. 2. a man who contributes tons of consistent pleasure and very little pain to a love relationship. 3. the perfect love match for you.

Over the years, the widespread popularity of movies like *Gone With the Wind, Pretty Woman, Romeo and Juliet, The Way We Were, Sleepless in Seattle, When Harry Met Sally, The Bridges of Madison County, Titanic, The American President,* and *My Big Fat Greek Wedding* have shown how much women dream of having a beautiful romance with a special kind of man.

But that brings up an interesting personal question: what exactly would it take for a man to be special to you?

THE SEXIEST MAN ALIVE AWARD

Every year *People Magazine* comes out with an issue that is titled "The Sexiest Man Alive." Past honorees include Mel Gibson, Mark Harmon, Harry Hamlin, Brad Pitt, the late John F. Kennedy, Jr., Sean Connery, Tom Cruise, Patrick Swayze, Nick Nolte, Harrison Ford, Denzel Washington, and George Clooney. In the year 2001 the honor of "The Sexiest Man Alive" went to actor Pierce Brosnan who currently plays the movie role of secret agent James Bond.

People Magazine described Brosnan as, "Suave and sophisticated, caring and kind, he's also a total knockout—and a one-woman man. Who wouldn't bond with this breathtaking Irishman?"

Pierce Brosnan seems to have it all. As a woman looking for a great relationship, rather than a mediocre one, you also want to find a man who has it all—that is, all the ingredients necessary to create a great love relationship with you.

A SIMPLE FISHING ANALOGY

In the sport of fishing, novice anglers dream of catching the biggest fish or the largest number of fish. But veteran anglers think much differently.

Tom Davis, author of *The Little Book of Fly-Fishing,* wrote, "The Basic Truths: The dimension of the reward is proportional to the size of the challenge, not the size of the fish. You've heard it before, but it's true—as anyone who has snaked a ten-incher out of an impossible spot will emphatically attest."

In fishing and in your love life, the size of the reward is proportional to the size of the important intangibles. Your ability to identify and accurately measure these intangibles becomes the secret to finding the "big one" for you.

THE BIG FISH EQUATION

Voltaire, the French writer (1694-1778), wrote, "Pleasure is the object, the duty, the goal of all rational creatures."

> "Everything you and I do, we do either out of our need to avoid pain or our desire to gain pleasure."
> Anthony Robbins
> Author of *Awaken the Giant Within* (1991)

On the other hand, an American proverb reminds us to "Always count the cost."

A wise person must both recognize this desire to seek pleasure and remember to weigh the costs.

For simplicity, you measure the size of your romantic love relationship by the amount of pleasure minus the amount of pain.

To illustrate this point more clearly, here are five relationship scenarios that you may encounter in your relationships with other people:

The Big One:	High pleasure/low pain
A Friend:	Medium pleasure/low pain
Acquaintances	Low pleasure/low pain
Crazy Love	High pleasure/high pain
The Enemy	Low pleasure/high pain

The big fish is the one who contributes consistent high levels of pleasure (happiness) and only occasional low levels of pain (misery) to your relationship.

DECIDE EXACTLY WHAT YOU WANT TO CATCH

So what do you look for in a man that would clue you in on potential pleasure and pain over time?

> "Boyfriends weren't friends at all; they were prizes, escorts, symbols of achievement, fascinating strangers, the Other."
>
> Susan Allen Toth
> Author of *Blooming* (1981)

If you observe closely and evaluate wisely, there are some intelligent ways to see through the clever disguises of elusive men. Here are some helpful suggestions on what to look for:

☝ **Start with a winner, not a loser.** A person with winning traits is the only one who will be capable of delivering consistent pleasure and very little pain. Remember that all big fish are winners. Don't waste your precious time, energy, and emotion on long-shot losers. Their excuses of bad luck rarely change.

☝ **Monitor your pulse, not just your purse.** A Greek proverb reads, "Love can not grow without passion." If a man doesn't drive your passion, you have no chance at the big romance, even if he has a fat wallet. Remember to go for a man who turns you on, not off. There is no substitute for chemistry.

☝ **Aim for character rather than "a character."** Men can be very charming with their manly strengths and boyish personalities. But underneath a man's charm lies a foundation of character. If consistent, lasting, and fulfilling love is your objective, character is one of your only reliable indicators.

☝ **Seek a warm heart, not a cold shoulder.** An undeniable and mysterious part of us seems to be attracted to cool, aloof people. But if you want a relationship with warmth, caring, sensitivity, and compassion, be sure that the ones you want also possess these vital emotional qualities for love. A man can only give away to you what he possesses inside.

☝ **Find a lifestyle match, not a mismatch.** Even the most charming, attractive, and exciting men may not be right for you. If you don't have similar values and lifestyles, differences may start to accumulate,

Let's face it, when an attractive but ALOOF ("cool") man comes along, there are some of us who offer to shine his shoes with our underpants. If he has a mean streak, somehow this is "attractive." There are thousands of scientific concepts as to why this is so, and yes, yes, it's very sick---but none of this helps.

Lynda Barry, American writer & cartoonist
from *An Uncommon Scold* by Abby Adams
(1989)

deepen, and widen. Remember that opposites may attract initially, but tend to repel consistently over time. In the long-run, similar values and lifestyle habits create the most secure and lasting relationship bonds. So while differences may be welcomed in style (and create some interesting relationship blends), they are not in substance.

⊛ **Select a personality complement, not a clash.** There's no denying that everyone enjoys the company of an interesting person with a so-called "good personality." However some personalities will blend better with yours than others. Repeated personality conflict usually means a large amount of emotional pain. Choose harmony instead of conflict in a loving relationship if you truly want secure, long-term, and consistent happiness.

There is nothing simple about men whether it is trying to catch them or understand them. But an intelligent approach to defining exactly what you want and what you don't want will lead you in the right direction toward love and happiness and away from pain and suffering.

Make Smart Decisions In Advance

Carol Botwin, author of *Tempted Women*, advised, "Pick a man for his qualities, his values, and his compatibility with you, rather than what he represents in terms of status, power, or good looks."

The challenge is to make your evaluations early in the relationship, before you get emotionally involved. Otherwise,

The Big Fish Test

ARE YOU HOOKED UP WITH THE MAN OF YOUR DREAMS?

Size up the man in your life. (Add up the score)

TALENT: HOW MUCH AM I ATTRACTED TO HIM?

- Physical appearance   Poor   Fair   Good   Excellent
- Intelligence & common sense   Poor   Fair   Good   Excellent
- Money/wealth/success   Poor   Fair   Good   Excellent

GAME: HOW WELL DOES HE CAPTURE MY ATTENTION?

- Sense of humor   Poor   Fair   Good   Excellent
- Confidence & personal power   Poor   Fair   Good   Excellent
- Conversational skill & charm   Poor   Fair   Good   Excellent

HEART: HOW MUCH DO I LIKE HIM?

- Emotional warmth & kindness   Poor   Fair   Good   Excellent
- Ability to listen & understand   Poor   Fair   Good   Excellent
- Sense of gratitude & appreciation   Poor   Fair   Good   Excellent

CHARACTER: HOW MUCH DO I RESPECT HIM?

- Responsibility/maturity   Poor   Fair   Good   Excellent
- Ability to handle adversity   Poor   Fair   Good   Excellent
- Honesty & integrity   Poor   Fair   Good   Excellent

FIT: HOW GOOD OF A TEAM DO WE MAKE?

- Shared human values   Poor   Fair   Good   Excellent
- Compatible lifestyle habits   Poor   Fair   Good   Excellent
- Harmonious personalities   Poor   Fair   Good   Excellent
- Matching relationship goals   Poor   Fair   Good   Excellent

Points:		Total Score:		
Excellent	4	53-64	The whopper
Good	3	40-52	A nice catch
Fair	2	26-39	Average size
Poor	0	0-25	Throw him back!

THE BOTTOM LINE:

Measure a man wisely by the size of his total package.

even the smartest women can end up in the dumbest romantic love relationships.

Remember, the secrets to your success in finding an ideal love partner are: 1) make intelligent evaluations, 2) concentrate your energies on the right man and the best situation for you, 3) think in terms of your long-term happiness, and 4) always do the right thing.

> "There are games and manipulations to make someone love you and want to marry you, but this doesn't ensure that he or she is right for you."
>
> John Gray
> Author of *Mars and Venus on a Date* (1997)

If you follow these guidelines, you will stop wasting time being faked out by the small suitors. That will leave you with more time and energy to focus on what you truly want and need: an attractive man that you like and respect with lots of game, plenty of heart, and who fits nicely into your life.

THE BOTTOM LINE

Men are like fish. Don't let the small ones grab your attention and steal your bait. Concentrate on catching only the bigger ones. You rarely get any better than what you aim for. Be smart, be patient, and aim high.

* Size up the men in your love life by taking "The Big Fish Test" on the opposite page and by reading "A Word About the Big Fish Test" on page 195. Learn the secrets to measuring a man's love value to you more accurately and wisely.

Twelve

Fishing Holes

INVEST YOUR TIME IN THE BEST SPOTS

Most of the world is covered by water.
A fisherman's job is simple:
Pick out the best parts.

Charles F. Waterman
Author of *Modern Fresh and Salt Water Fly Fishing* (1975)

fish•ing holes: 1. small areas of a lake, river, or stream where fish congregate or feed. 2. high-percentage places for catching fish. 3. where to meet the men you want.

Have you ever found yourself, like the country song says, "looking for love in all the wrong places?"

Dr. Joy Browne, a radio talk-show host and author of *Dating For Dummies*, wrote, "If you're hanging out at Joe's Pub or sitting on your fanny in front of the tube, the perfect date—someone who lights your fire, rings your chimes, or at least doesn't make you nauseous—is going to remain the stuff of fantasy instead of reality."

If you want to meet the right man for your love life, then you will have to start looking (fishing) for love in all the "right" places instead.

MY LOW-PERCENTAGE SINGLES' BAR

For many single men and women, the bar or club scene is a popular and convenient way to meet members of the opposite sex. But like a lot of strategies, there is a smart way and a dumb way to go about it.

A favorite hangout of mine is a place called *Panama Joe's Cantina* in Long Beach, California. I had been going there regularly for the last eight or nine years.

One day it occurred to me that in about a thousand or so visits to *Panama Joe's Cantina*, I'd only met one woman who I had any kind of a dating relationship with.

One in a thousand is not a very good percentage for meeting quality people. I would hate to go through another one thousand visits in order to find a second date.

> **"The best fisherman in the world can't catch them if they aren't there."**
> Anthony Acerrano
> Fishing editor of *Sports Afield*

While the bar scene may be a good place to spend an occasional evening listening to music or watching a sporting event on the big screen, it may not be the most intelligent choice to invest major social energies in the search for your ideal big romance.

When asked on the subject of going to bars to meet first-rate partners, Ann Landers, the syndicated columnist and author of *Wake Up and Smell the Coffee*, wrote, "If you want to catch trout, don't fish in a herring barrel."

In fishing and in your love life, always remember that you can't catch the ones you want if they are not where you are.

A SIMPLE FISHING ANALOGY

With today's modern technology, there is an electronic device for locating the exact position of deep-water fish called a fishfinder.

I was flipping through a fishing magazine at the dentist office when I came across a half-page advertisement that read: "*The ProFish II Fishfinder* brings big-league color fishfinding to the small boat, recreation fisherman. It does it first-class with features that include depth ranges up to 1500 feet, eight-level color signal processing, high-speed zoom,

A third of all romances start on the job.... Office romance is alive and well, despite a barrage of corporate counter-measures.... Between 6 million and 8 million Americans enter into a romance with a fellow employee each year....About half of all office romances evolve into lasting relationships or marriage.

U.S. News & World Report
December 14, 1998

graphical fairway guidance screens, car-like speedometer graphics, turbo-speed plotter redraw and more."

With the aid of one of these new fishfinder devices, an angler can effectively locate the position of the elusive big fish. That way smart anglers can fish in the very best spots.

In the sport of fishing and in your love life, make sure that you invest the majority of your time in the most likely areas for catching the ones you really want.

CREATE YOUR OWN ROMANCE OPPORTUNITIES

Dr. Natasha Josefowitz, author of *Paths of Power: A Woman's Guide From First Job to Top Executive*, wrote, "What is luck? It is not only chance, it is also creating the opportunity, recognizing it when it is there, and taking it when it comes."

> "When luck offers a finger one must
> take the whole hand."
> Swedish proverb

To help you get lucky in meeting your elusive "big fish," here are some valuable ideas to factor into your overall love strategy for men:

- ⊛ **Go where the big ones are.** Remember that all big fish are winners in life. So if you want to meet a winner, go to places where winners like to go. Keep in mind that most successful men "work hard, play hard, think hard, contribute their energy to worthwhile causes, and are well-connected." Use this as a guideline for mapping out places that you and your social fishing buddies can frequent more often.

Favorite Fishing Holes
101 Hot Spots Where the Big Ones are Biting!

(Big Fish: Work Hard, Play Hard, Think Hard, Contribute to Worthy Causes, Well Connected)

1. Attend a golf or tennis tournament
2. Attend a local college or high school football or basketball game
3. Play on a coed softball team
4. Enter a 10 K race and all the festivities
5. Take an aerobics, yoga, or exercise class
6. Hit some golf balls at the driving range
7. Find a popular jogging or cycling path
8. Learn to scuba dive, kayak or water-ski
9. Try your luck at the racetrack
10. Join an active & fun ski club
11. Go fishing at a popular place
12. Visit a boating or fishing trade show
13. Have lunch at the golf course
14. Go to Starbuck's and bring a newspaper
15. Have lunch at an outdoor sidewalk cafe
16. Go out for Monday Night Football
17. Go to a sushi bar or piano bar
18. Eat lunch where businessmen go
19. Take a first aid or CPR training
20. Find a pub with an outgoing bartender
21. Have lunch in a museum's cafe
22. Support your local charity's pancake breakfast or casino night
23. Have lunch at the best deli in town
24. Go to a Club Med Village for singles
25. Go skiing on President's Day weekend
26. Take a 3-day weekend cruise vacation
27. Fly in the business-class section
28. Go to a karaoke singing night
29. Live, eat, bank & shop where singles do
30. Go to church singles' events
31. Take a "start your own business" class
32. Attend a "singles' only" dance or mixer
33. Try an online dating service
34. Visit a winery for a tasting and tour
35. Take a ferry, train, subway, or boat ride
36. Take a city tour or day trip in your own or nearby city (history or architecture)
37. Take continuing education courses
38. Take a computer or Internet class
39. Go to an investment seminar
40. Go to your town's annual parade early
41. Take a 1-day time-management course
42. Go to business breakfasts and luncheons to hear good speakers
43. Meet with co-workers for "Happy Hour" after work with good free food
44. Take a "Fear of Flying" seminar
45. Get invited to some Christmas parties
46. Attend a friend or co-worker's wedding
47. Go to a high school or college reunion
48. Go to an adults-only Halloween party
49. Throw a barbecue party in the summer
50. Go to a good Super Bowl party
51. Attend your kids soccer games
52. Attend your kid's school functions
53. Go to concerts early and meet others
54. Go to a hair saloon that caters to both men and women clients
55. Listen to a live outdoor jazz concert
56. Grocery shop on weekends or evenings
57. Take your dog for a walk in the park
58. Shop in a gourmet, wine or health foods store like Whole Foods Market
59. Share a cab fare with someone
60. Shop for sporting goods or computers
61. Go to the car wash on a busy weekend
62. Go to the best Sunday brunch spot
63. Learn how to play craps at a casino
64. Browse for used CD's at a music store
65. Go to the zoo, circus, or aquarium
66. Browse home improvement stores like Home Depot and Lowe's
67. Attend your local radio or television station's promotional events
68. Join a booster club at your local college
69. Take an evening class at a local college
70. Take a woodworking or handyman class
71. Teach a workshop that caters to men
72. Go backpacking or white-water rafting
73. Shop at Eddie Bauer or Sharper Image
74. Frequent the Barnes & Noble or Borders Books magazine section
75. Photograph men playing sports
76. Go to art gallery openings
77. Go to plays at the community theater
78. Go to a car auction or classic car show
79. Join a local toastmasters club
80. Take photos of men with their dogs
81. Attend "neighborhood watch" meetings
82. Volunteer for a political fund-raiser
83. Go with a friend to a bowling alley
84. Attend a variety of social events around the Valentine's Day theme
85. Go to a chili cook-off contest
86. Take a dance class (swing or salsa)
87. Go to the best microbrewery in town
88. Visit the local stock brokerage house
89. Stay at a hotel with all the amenities
90. Attend civic meetings on key issues
91. Get involved in an office football pool
92. Go to Chamber of Commerce functions
93. Take part in an Earth Day event
94. Go to a performance driving school
95. Assist with a youth organization
96. Join a ladies golf group
97. Help gather signatures for a petition
98. Go to a polo match
99. Take a martial arts class
100. Find a popular snowmobile area
101. Watch an evening men's softball game

116

- Ⓨ **Go where the big ones are biting**. People are most approachable when their guard is down and they are deeply involved in an activity. Look for stimulating activities that are centered around things like sports, entertainment, worthwhile causes, education, travel, friends, family, church, home, or work. You can meet people more naturally around an activity than you can by direct effort. (For more specific ideas, check out the "101 Favorite Fishing Holes" on the opposite page.)

- Ⓨ **Go to places with great atmosphere**. Standing in a long line at the Department of Motor Vehicles is one of the most unpleasant environments. On the other hand, taking an afternoon stroll along a sandy beach in Maui might put someone in a fabulous mood. Atmosphere is one of the intangibles that has a powerful effect on how well people interact. Look for places that have stimulating or aesthetically pleasing atmospheres to help you meet people in the most favorable moods.

- Ⓨ **Cultivate your own backyard**. Don't discount the importance of proximity. The "big one" you've been dreaming about may be standing outside in your own proverbial backyard. Since the majority of your time is spent where you live or work, the odds are that you'll be more likely to meet people there. We tend to think that someone special will appear in only magical settings. But more often than not, opportunity comes disguised in plain clothes, normal activities, and everyday surroundings.

117

- ℘ **Expand your social networks.** An effective way to meet people is by personal referrals. Your friends, family, and business associates can be valuable sources of social opportunities if you're willing to ask for their help. By tapping into your social networks, you can greatly increase your number of quality social opportunities. Ironically, the best way for some women to meet a man is to meet another woman....an enlightened friend who can make a smooth love connection for her.

- ℘ **Try something new.** Sometimes a healthy break from your regular life may be the stimulus you need to kick-start your love life. The ideal partner for you may be similar in some ways, but unique in others. (For insight on the new online dating craze, turn to page 196 for "Internet Dating Strategies.")

- ℘ **Take a vacation for faster action.** A major drawback to falling in love with someone on vacation is the pain associated with long-distance romances that result in either shattered fantasies or major relocations. But if it's exciting action that you crave, few things can top a steamy vacation romance. However if you choose to indulge, remember to handle these love affairs with the utmost caution.

- ℘ **Some men are not so hard to catch as they are hard to reach.** Expand your search for men beyond your comfort zone with the understanding that some quality men are hard for women to reach. Find some good fishing buddies who will take you to out-of-the-way places where these men are swimming around with their emotional guards down.

A Chinese proverb reads, "Intelligence consists in recognizing opportunity." Get clear on what you want, go to the best meeting places, and engage in the right kinds of activities. Then you will have an easier time recognizing and anticipating your most promising prospects for love.

INVEST YOUR PRECIOUS TIME IN THE BEST SPOTS

Woody Allen, the actor, writer, and filmmaker said, "Eighty percent of success is showing up."

If you want the probabilities to work in your favor, spend the majority of your social time in the best meeting spots for the high-quality men you want. Then when your opportunity for love eventually comes around, be sure to pull the trigger and follow through with the appropriate interactions.

Success at meeting the right kind of men is simply a matter of playing the numbers game more intelligently.

If you want to improve your luck at meeting the man of your dreams, go to a variety of the right places, at the ideal times, with your most supportive fishing buddies, and in the freshest physical and emotional state.

THE BOTTOM LINE

Men are like fish. If you consistently cast an attractive bait into a high-percentage fishing hole, you'll eventually get a good strike from a big fish. Men can rarely resist the temptation of attractive, available, and lively feminine bait.

BALLARD STREET   Jerry Van Amerongen

Thirteen

The Crowds

OUTPOSITION YOUR COMPETITION

Even though competition has no place in fly-fishing, and should be none, the angler ought to strive always to play a good game. He should practice the tactics of his art with the same zeal as do the followers of competitive sports if he hopes ever to become an expert fly-fisherman in the highest sense of that much misused term.

George La Branche
Author of *The Dry Fly and Fast Water* (1914)

crowd: 1. a large group of people confined in a restricted area. 2. your competition for catching the elusive big fish. 3. in the context of finding and meeting desirable eligible men to date, almost all other single women.

If you find yourself in a mountain forest being pursued by an angry grizzly bear, are your chances of escaping better by running uphill or downhill?

The answer is neither. The grizzly bear can easily catch you in either direction.

The best strategy for escaping an angry grizzly bear is to make sure that you bring along a much slower friend.

> "I don't have to be enemies with someone
> to be competitors with them."
> Jackie Joyner-Kersee
> American Olympic champion

The point I am trying to make is this: sometimes the difference in life between success and failure is merely a matter of being one up on your immediate competition.

Gelett Burgess, the American illustrator and author (1866-1951), wrote, "Most women have all other women as adversaries; most men have all other men as their allies."

One of the unfortunate realities of love and life is that competition is a force that has to be reckoned with from time-to-time. In the case of finding and dating the man who is regarded as the "romantic whopper," this can be especially true for single women.

A SIMPLE FISHING ANALOGY

According to the *USA Today* April 18, 1997 edition, "44 million people hooked on fishing spend billions...The National Sporting Goods Association ranks fishing with 44.2 million participants in 1995, as the nation's No. 5 favorite activity behind such universal standbys as walking, biking, swimming, and working out on gym equipment."

With the growing popularity of fishing in our country, it's common these days to find the shores of America's lakes and streams overcrowded with eager anglers.

> "Crowded Waters: There are times when the promise of fast, furious action—and, especially, the promise of big fish—eclipses aesthetic concerns.
>
> Tom Davis
> Author of *The Little Book of Fly-Fishing* (1997)

In order to fish effectively today, anglers must learn to not only outsmart the fish, but they also must outsmart the other fishermen. Otherwise, he or she is more likely to spend the bulk of the day tangling up their fishing lines with other anglers instead of catching the big fish.

For success in the sport of fishing and in your love life, be sure you know how to deal effectively with crowds.

YOU CAN'T WIN THEM ALL!

One winter I went to Idaho for the *Annual Sun Valley Singles' Ski Week*. On the first night of that vacation I met an attractive young woman named Deanna, who I shared some fun dancing and bar-hopping moments with.

The next day I got together with Deanna for another night on the town. As our taxi pulled onto Main Street in downtown Sun Valley, we saw a large sign hanging outside one of the bars that read, "Hot Jeans Contest Tonight."

Deanna said, "I'd like to enter that contest."

We got out of the cab, went inside the bar, and joined the wild crowd. Deanna entered the "Hot Jeans Contest," won her preliminary round, and advanced to the finals.

As the final round was about to begin, the announcer said on the loudspeaker, "And now, help me bring up our celebrity judge for the final round, Mr. Clint Eastwood."

The crowd roared with approval as Clint took a seat up front with the other judges. Deanna was one of six contestants. When the Hot Jeans Contest was over, Deanna had come in a disappointing fifth place.

After the results were announced, Deanna and I were standing around the bar when none other than Clint Eastwood came by. He looked at Deanna and said in his distinctive, masculine voice, "I gave you all the points I could."

Deanna gave Clint a big hug and a kiss.

I reached out my hand and said, "Hi, Clint. My name is Steve Nakamoto."

He mumbled back something like, "whatever."

I stood around for a few minutes before I realized that I was the odd man out in the conversation. I excused myself, thinking that I would hook up with Deanna later in the evening. But that was not to be the case. From that moment on, Clint and Deanna were off on their own together.

I consoled myself with the thought that Deanna must have had a tough choice: Clint Eastwood (*People Weekly's* 2001 #2

most popular screen actor of all time) or Steve Nakamoto?
It could have gone either way, right?

> **"The strategy to use depends on which rung
> you occupy on the ladder."**
> Al Ries and Jack Trout
> Authors of *The 22 Immutable Laws of Marketing* (1993)

Sometimes competition for the opposite sex is an issue that you have to deal with, whether you like it or not. The most that you can do is give each competitive encounter your best shot and let the chips fall where they may. You can't expect to win them all.

OUTPOSITION THE COMPETITION

In their book, *Positioning: The Battle For Your Mind,* business consultants Al Ries and Jack Trout discuss strategies for marketing products or services so they get "positioned" in the forefront of the buyer's mind.

To help position yourself in the forefront of a man's mind, here are some important guidelines to consider:

- ☙ **Be first.** Being first is the simplest way to position yourself ahead of the competition. Those who wait only get what is left. Find out what you want and slip in ahead of the crowd.

- ☙ **Size up your competition.** Battles are more easily won when your strengths are matched up against your rival's weaknesses. Be smart and only compete when the match-ups tilt more favorably in your favor. Otherwise, don't compete at all.

125

The Fishing Buddy Test

HOW GOOD IS THE COMPANY YOU'RE ANGLING WITH?

(Circle Your Choices & Add Up The Score)

LOVE FOR THE SPORT

• Physical Energy	Poor	Fair	Good	Excellent
• Enthusiasm & Optimism	Poor	Fair	Good	Excellent
• Fun & Sense of Humor	Poor	Fair	Good	Excellent
• Attitude Toward Men	Poor	Fair	Good	Excellent
• Willingness To Try New Places	Poor	Fair	Good	Excellent

SHARING THE SUGAR

• Shares the Attention	Poor	Fair	Good	Excellent
• Shares the Good Prospects	Poor	Fair	Good	Excellent
• Shares the Conversation	Poor	Fair	Good	Excellent
• Appreciates Your Unique Gifts	Poor	Fair	Good	Excellent
• Sells You When You're Absent	Poor	Fair	Good	Excellent

BUDDY BONUS POINTS

• Matching Moral Values	Poor	Fair	Good	Excellent
• Will Defend Your Backside	Poor	Fair	Good	Excellent
• Keeps Your Standards High	Poor	Fair	Good	Excellent
• Brings Out The Best In You	Poor	Fair	Good	Excellent
• Common Sense	Poor	Fair	Good	Excellent

Points:			Total Score:		
Excellent	4		51-60	A Great Sport
Good	3		41-50	Good Tag-Along
Fair	2		31-40	Not Much Help
Poor	0		0-30	Leave 'em Home!

THE BOTTOM LINE:

Enjoy the sport of fishing for love by selecting a variety of great angling (male and female) buddies. It's much easier to be both patient and persistent when you're having fun.

*For more insight on this subject, turn to page 197 for "Your Best Fishing Buddies"

ⓥ **Find Your Niche.** If you can't be the best in one category, then be the best in another category. You can
outshine your competition, for example, by being
sharper, wiser, kinder, stronger, more confident,
more passionate, or a better listener. The battle of
talents has predictable results: the one with the
most talent always wins. Shift the playing field onto
one of your other areas (heart or character) of
strengths. Fight your key battles there instead.

ⓥ **Outclass your rivals.** Rise above petty competition.
Don't get caught up in putting down your rivals. If
you can't compete with class, choose not to compete at all. Maintain your integrity and dignity. The
classy manner in which you play the game of love
also gets noticed and appreciated by the more
enlightened and mature fish (men).

ⓥ **Defend yourself against attackers.** Learn to shield
and defend yourself from unfriendly attacks.
Realize that some people build themselves up by
tearing others down. Don't let them do that to you.
If you want others to respect you, be sure to respect
yourself by standing firm against unfriendly, intentional, inappropriate, and excessive verbal attacks.

ⓥ **Make good alliances.** One of the best ways to disarm
your rivals is by associating yourself with good
angling buddies. These friends can support and
protect you from the unkind attacks of your competition. (See the opposite page for selecting the
best buddies to go angling for love with.)

DON'T TAKE ANYTHING PERSONALLY

Nothing others do is because of you. What others say and do is a projection of their own reality, their own dream. When you are immune to the opinions and actions of others, you won't be the victim of needless suffering.

Don Miguel Ruiz
Author of *The Four Agreements* (1997)

Dealing effectively with competition is about becoming the best you can be and marketing yourself in the most creative and advantageous ways.

REMEMBER THAT IT ONLY TAKES ONE!

Aristotle Onassis, the legendary billionaire Greek financier (1906-1975), said, "The secret of business is to know something that nobody else knows."

Knowing how to "position" effectively will tilt the odds of success in your favor. Even though you may lose an occasional battle, you'll get more than enough chances to come out ahead in the long run.

> "He that wrestles with us strengthens our nerves and sharpens our skill. Our antagonist is our helper."
>
> Edmund Burke
> British statesman (1729-1797)

While the saying goes, "There are plenty of fish in the sea," in the sport of love, you only need one in order to succeed.

Learn to deal effectively with competition. You will eliminate a major hindrance to your love life and free-up more of your creative social energy on what's really most important: the art of catching the elusive big fish.

THE BOTTOM LINE

Men are like fish. The big fish naturally attract a larger crowd. Your chances for success lie in establishing the best possible position against your competition. Handle your areas of weakness, but win your battles with your strengths.

IN THE BLEACHERS
By Steve Moore

Fish horror stories.

Fourteen

The Cast

DON'T SPOOK AWAY MEN WITH BAD APPROACHES

It is not easy to tell one how to cast.
The art must be acquired by practice.

Charles Orvis
Author of *Fishing with a Fly* (1883)
from
Well-Cast Lines by John Merwin

cast: 1. the act of throwing your fishing line and bait into the water. 2. a well-planned approach to your target fish. 3. how to become more effective at meeting the men you want.

Letty Cottin Pogrebin, best-selling author of *Down With Sexist Upbringing*, wrote, "Boys don't make passes at female smart asses."

If you want quality men to make a good "pass" at you, develop an effective style of approaching them or getting noticed. Some women can slip into almost any social situation quickly and easily. However, others are more apt to scare men away early with bad or awkward approaches.

Remember that you usually only get one chance at the elusive big fish so make sure your initial approach is a good one.

A SIMPLE FISHING ANALOGY

The word for "approach" in the sport of fishing is "cast." Learning to cast properly means to position your bait within striking range of the fish without spooking him away.

> "I wanted to be interested in and knowledgeable about one thing. I wanted to learn not to frighten a trout in the water."
>
> Gretchen Legler
> Author of *All the Powerful Invisible Things* (1995)

According to the fly-fishing guidebook, *The Curtis Creek Manifesto*, by Sheridan Anderson, "Frightened fish can't be caught! Heavy duty fish frighteners include: vibration, carnivores (if you can see the fish, they can see you), shadows, strange movements—even your tip, other scared fish, a sloppy cast, lunkers, indiscreet pick-up, etc., and so forth. You can't avoid scaring some of the fish, but the less you scare, the more you catch."

In fishing and in your love life, the only fish you can catch are the ones you don't scare away. Be sure your approaches are natural, well-conceived, and beautifully performed.

THE WEEKEND "FUN" CRUISE TO MEXICO

Every weekend the *M.S. Ecstacy* sails out of Los Angeles to Ensenada, Mexico. It is a three-day cruise that is filled with good times and a chance to hook-up with a little romance.

Things happen quickly on this cruise. The first night is called "Get Acquainted Night." The second night is "The Captain's Gala Dinner." And the third night is "The Farewell Party." In spite of the short amount of time, people make good friendships, and in some cases, lasting romances.

One of the main reasons people hit it off so well is that there are several easy opportunities to meet people.

> "The best way to meet people is to do what you love to do. Activity is the most natural and comfortable way to make contact."
> Steve Bhaerman and Don McMillan
> Authors of *Friends & Lovers* (1996)

You can naturally meet people during the fire boat drill, dancing in the disco, gambling in the casino, dining in the restaurant, grabbing a seat for the show, sipping a tropical drink at cocktail hour, taking the excursion bus, lounging by the pool, playing a game of shuffleboard, strolling on the decks, or mixing it up at the Singles' Mingle Party.

With a few helpful pointers, almost anyone can have a great time making new friends. It is during these activities that anything can happen, including romance.

The art of approaching people on the *M.S. Ecstacy* weekend cruise is nothing more than catching people off-guard, sharing a good time, and making a favorable first impression.

We could just as easily take the stress out of meeting new people by using this same casual attitude and approach in our normal day-to-day social lives.

MAKE A GREAT FIRST IMPRESSION

A popular American saying goes, "You only get one chance at making a good first impression."

Numerous studies show how in only a few seconds, people clearly decide whether you are a "yes," "no," or "maybe." With this in mind, here are some pointers to help you avoid being an automatic "no" in the minds of the men you want:

- **Be approachable.** Create space and make it inviting for men to meet you. Do your best to give off non-verbal signals that suggest your interest in meeting and talking with someone. A warm and receptive smile on your face is a good place to start.

- **Start with unconscious rapport.** People can create unconscious bonds through non-verbal communication. A word that describes this bonding process is "rapport." Michael Brooks, a communications expert and the author of *Instant Rapport*, wrote:

134

"People primarily experience the world through one of three senses: sight, sound, or feeling. By being aware of a person's gestures, breathing patterns, eye movements, and language, you can pinpoint his or her particular sensory preference. And armed with this knowledge, you can take charge: Match your communication style—whether it's visual, auditory, or kinesthetic—to that of another and become instantly more persuasive, effective, and even lovable."

☙ **Break the ice easily.** Find non-threatening topics to get your conversations started quickly and easily. Remind yourself that the best conversations are mostly pleasant in nature. Play it safe initially by avoiding sensitive subjects like politics, religion, money, and sex. Those kinds of issues can wait until you know the other person a little better.

☙ **Show him you care.** A Japanese proverb reads, "One kind word can warm three winter months." People are more interested in how much you care about them than in how much you know. Show them how much you care by your examples of thoughtfulness, kindness, sincerity, respect, and compassion.

☙ **Remember his name.** Dale Carnegie, author of *How to Win Friends and Influence People*, wrote, "If you remember my name, you pay me a subtle compliment; you indicate that I have made an impression on you. Remember my name and you add to my feelings of importance." Like a warm smile, remem-

Move things off-center with
a non-threatening
question. The best ice-
breaker in this age of every-
body moving around is:
Where are you from?
Geography is the most
neutral of subjects, but is
pregnant with
conversation possibilities. It
opens up a whole range of
secondary questions, allows
you to compare
impressions of places
where you've been, and
prompts you to explain
how you come to be where
you are. More than that
depends on chemistry.

Glen Waggoner and Peggy Maloney
Authors of *Esquire Etiquette* (1987)

bering a person's name is one of the simplest, yet most effective ways to make a good first impression.

⊚ **Avoid the conversation killers.** If you want to keep a conversation alive, don't: criticize, complain, condemn, argue, interrupt, confront, finish other's sentences, put down others, insist on your views, or dwell on negative subjects. Seek areas of agreement rather than areas of disagreement. Save your heated debates for the appropriate political arenas.

⊚ **Eliminate annoying mannerisms and sayings.** Some seemingly harmless things can drive men away. You might want to be more careful about rolling your eyes back with disapproval or the repeated use of a tired worn-out phrase like "been there, done that."

⊚ **Get him to play.** If you can get people to laugh at themselves, you almost automatically become their friend. Remember that most people are naturally cautious. If you can find creative playful ways to get them to lower their guard or lighten up, you're well on your way to a mutually enjoyable interaction.

⊚ **Disarm him with compliments.** Oscar Wilde, the Irish playwright (1854-1900), wrote, "Women are never disarmed by compliments. Men always are. That is the difference between the sexes." One of the best ways to move a man emotionally is to keep him off-balance with a timely and tasteful compliment. Try either his positive character traits (honesty, sincerity, caring) or his taste in what he wears (neckties, shirts, fabrics) or owns (cars, collections).

Why Men Don't Call Back!

Here's a list of some common ways that women spook away men early. It also reveals how some men can judge the women they date unfairly. While this list may upset overly sensitive women, it can also provide valuable feedback for enlightened anglers wishing to land the big one or for women who want to get rid of a bothersome small fish. Unless you get the man hooked or smitten early, many of these items will send him swimming away fast.

* Any outward signs of bitterness or anger toward men
* Have him see you being rude to waiters and waitresses
* Drive a clunker, live in a dump, or dress like a slob
* Have too many cats or big dogs running around your small place
* Have a strange laugh, a weird sense of humor, or laugh at the wrong time
* Be emotionally high-strung, get hysterical, or be high-maintenance
* Be highly opinionated or voice a strong, unpopular prejudice
* Be too much of a character or have an unflattering nickname
* Gossip excessively or share your dating exploits indiscriminately
* Express with wild gestures and overly dramatic facial expressions
* Refer often to past lovers especially violent, jealous ones
* Insist on telling long uninterrupted (boring) personal stories
* Eat like a horse, be a noisy eater, or show bad table manners
* Constantly interrupting people with unsolicited advice
* Get easily offended, argue excessively, or create a public scene
* Be too much of a sports jock, be too competitive, or be too manly
* Order expensive items off of the menu (fine wine, dessert, lobster, etc.)
* Cuss, swear, or get angry like a guy in public
* Have a bad job or be unemployed for too long of a time
* Own too many credit cards or come across as a big-time shopper
* Be sarcastic, cynical, condescending, or too much of a smart-ass
* Clash with a guy's best friends or close family members
* Call him too frequently and leave long dull messages
* Be too bossy and tell other people what they should do or think
* Have no friends and appear lonely, desperate, or needy
* Have him see old pictures of you when you were not very attractive
* Say "I love you" before the thought ever occurs to him
    (For a more complete "spooking" analysis, turn to pages 198-203)

⊗ **Make him fear a lost opportunity.** Men absolutely hate or fear the feeling of rejection. Make sure that men know you are available for dating. The best kind of availability, however, is limited availability. If you're never available, men will think you're already involved or not interested. But if you're available all the time, they'll think there must be something wrong with you. The best strategy is to be somewhere in the middle. Make the man fear a lost opportunity more than being rejected.

To approach others effortlessly or to be comfortably approached by others is the essence of "casting." It is a difficult skill that gets easier with practice and honest feedback.

> "Opportunity only knocks once."
> English proverb

The important thing to remind yourself before you cast your line is that a frightened fish (man) can't be caught. Learn to cast effectively and you will have lots of men swimming around to check out your alluring feminine bait.

The Bottom Line

Men are like fish. They can get spooked easily by the slightest negative vibe. Learn not to scare them away early by making your initial impressions nothing less than outstanding.

* Take a look at the opposite page for some of the more common "spooking" occurrences and page 204 to learn about the vital skill of "How to Catch a Man Off-Guard."

IN THE BLEACHERS

By Steve Moore

Fifteen

The Snags

BEWARE OF THE HIDDEN OBSTACLES

There is not a fly-fisherman on earth,
no matter how skilled, who has not
been humbled by a low-hanging
branch or a submerged boulder.

Judy Muller
Author of "A Woman's Place," *Home Waters: A Fly-Fishing
Anthology,* edited by Gary Soucie (1991)

snags: 1. hidden or unseen obstacles and barriers 2. the negative emotions that drive love away from you. 3. the illusions of debilitating fear and self-doubt that can be removed entirely by human courage and compassion.

In our love lives, we can encounter serious obstacles, whether they are real or imagined, that get in the way of the love we so deeply want and need.

> **"Without love our life is...like a ship without a rudder...like a body without a soul."**
> Shalom Aleichem
> Russian-born humorist (1859-1916)

To prevent this from happening, we must first identify the obstacles to love and then either avoid or remove them completely from our lives.

What we all want is a clear path to love.

A SIMPLE FISHING ANALOGY

In the sport of fishing, a snag is an underwater obstacle, like a sunken tree limb or a large rock, that catches or tangles an angler's fishing line.

Tony Whieldon, author of *The Complete Guide to Fishing Skills*, wrote, "There's always a risk of snagging your line on an underwater obstruction. If you know the position of an obstruction, hold the float back harder than normal so that the hookbait will swing up and over the snag. Having an intimate knowledge of an area suddenly helps you avoid snags.

Wear sunglasses, which cut out the surface glare and allow you to see objects more clearly under the water."

In the sport of fishing and in your love life, beware of the hidden or submerged obstacles. Don't let snags prevent your attractive bait from reaching your desired target.

Avoid The Impossible Love Obstacles

When I was in high school, I had a crush on a girl named Patty who lived in my neighborhood. Almost every evening she would stop by my house and we would walk her German shepherd dog around the block together. At first we were just good friends. But before long, we were holding hands and finding secret places to kiss.

My problem was that her father wouldn't let me take her out on a date because of his prejudice against my Japanese heritage. At first we tried our best to sneak around him, but eventually the weight of the hassles broke us apart.

> "Every obstacle is for the best."
> Greek proverb

At that young age, there was nothing we could have done to correct the situation. Her father's disapproval of me was an obstacle that should have been avoided completely. But I was only sixteen years old and didn't know any better.

A word to the wise: There are some obstacles, like pursuing married game, that are better off being avoided altogether, rather than challenged.

Become a smart angler. Recognize and avoid all the impossible love situations. There are better places to invest your precious romantic energies.

ALWAYS DO YOUR BEST

Your best is going to change
from moment to moment;
it will be different when you
are healthy as opposed to
sick. Under any circum-
stance, simply do your best,
and you will avoid self-judg-
ment, self-abuse, and regret.

Don Miguel Ruiz
Author of *The Four Agreements* (1997)

REMOVE YOUR EMOTIONAL OBSTACLES

On the other hand, emotional obstacles which only exist in your mind are the hurdles that need to be removed, not avoided. These obstacles only prevent you from taking the important actions that you need to make in order to create your desired love outcome.

Until you remove these obstacles, love may pass you by in spite of your abundant talent and skill in other areas of love. To avoid missing out on love, here are some major emotional obstacles to locate and remove from your life entirely:

- ☞ **Disguised Anger: A**ngry anglers catch no fish! Start by eliminating all sources of residual bitterness, envy, and cynicism. The snag of anger will prevent your otherwise attractive feminine bait from ever being properly appreciated by prospective big fish.

- ☞ **Excessive Frustration.** One of the realities of life is that you don't succeed every time. Don't let your frustration damage the quality of your attempts. In order to succeed at love, each attempt at love must be optimistic, confident, and fresh.

- ☞ **Fear of Failure.** Marilyn Ferguson, author of *The Aquarian Conspiracy,* wrote, "Ultimately, we know deeply that the other side of every fear is a freedom." Be willing to take a chance. If you want what you truly desire, be sure to aim high. Realize that aiming high means you will occasionally get less than wonderful outcomes. Accept these results as an equal trade-off for the freedom to choose who and what you really want in your love life.

ʘ **Fear of Rejection.** If someone says "no" to your advances, it's either a sign to ask again, ask at another time, ask in another way, or ask someone else instead. Sometimes your best prospects are no more than prospects. Give each opportunity your best shot and if the response is not favorable enough, move on. Realize that if you're not right for them, then they're certainly not right for you.

ʘ **Lack of Courage.** A Philippine proverb reads, "Courage beats the enemy." You can beat your fears by simply taking decisive action. Don't let your mood at the moment stop you from the actions that you know are the right things to do. Realize that it is often only the first step that is difficult. The rest of your actions are much easier to take once you establish some positive momentum.

ʘ **Lack of Persistence.** When nothing seems to help, picture a stonecutter hammering away at his rock, perhaps a hundred times without as much as a crack showing in it. Yet at the hundredth and first blow it will split in two, and you'll know it wasn't that last blow that did it but all the hammering that had gone on before.

ʘ **Lack of Faith.** Comete de Buffon, the French naturalist (1707-1788), wrote, "Never think that God's delays are God's denials. Hold on; hold fast; hold out. Patience is genius." You hear a lot about a lack of commitment, but behind this fear is the broader issue of a lack of faith. Faith is simply the absolute knowing that consistent good actions eventually translate into good results. Realize that the rewards in your life can often be delayed and indirect.

Many of these obstacles in their milder forms are simple warnings for us to prepare for action. But in their "excessive" form, these emotional obstacles prevent us from the positive actions that we would ordinarily take.

OBSTACLES ARE ONLY ILLUSIONS

Dr. Wayne Dyer, best-selling author of *Your Erroneous Zones* and *The Sky's the Limit,* wrote, "The only block to your happiness is your belief that you have blocks."

The obstacles or blocks that you may sense are only an illusion. When you muster up the courage, take congruent action, and keep persevering, you are effectively removing the imaginary emotional obstacles from your life.

> **"A clear understanding of negative emotions dismisses them."**
> Vernon Howard
> Author of *Esoteric Mind Power* (1973)

Opportunities for love only become available to you after you've cleared the way by avoiding or removing the debilitating snags in your love life.

THE BOTTOM LINE

The obstacles of your love life can be removed by the strength of your character. Don't ever let fear stand in your way of love and happiness. When you are faced with a challenge, be sure to respond with courageous, decisive action.

SINGLE SLICES   by Peter Kohlsaat

Sixteen

The Nibbles

GAUGE YOUR EARLY RESPONSES WISELY

He (she) that will be an expert angler
must be endured with the following
qualifications: PATIENCE, DILIGENCE,
and RESOLUTION. Patience to endure
the disappointment that attends
anglers; diligence in observing the
various seasons of the year, and
various dispositions of fish; resolute,
to rise early, and pursue his (her) sport,
whether it be hot or cold,
in winter or summer.

The Angler's Guide (1828)
from
The Angler's Quotation Book by Eric Restall

nib•bles: 1. small or hesitant bites on your fishing line. 2. the early relationship phase of getting to know a man a little bit at a time. 3. a process designed to evaluate potential mates.

An age-old English proverb reads, "Do not judge the size of the ship from the land."

In our love lives, we often try to evaluate the future size of a love relationship based on sketchy first impressions. If we like the first impression, then we are more inclined to take another closer look at the other person so we can make a more accurate judgment as to the potential of the hook-up.

This process of getting to know another person better and sizing up their potential in a romantic love relationship is something we commonly refer to as "dating."

A Simple Fishing Analogy

In the sport of fishing, when a fish takes a small bite out of a piece of bait it's called a "nibble." Some fish bite lightly, others more firmly, and still others like to grab and run.

Since anglers can rarely see under the water's surface, the best they can do is gauge the quality of the nibble by the strength of the tug on the fishing line.

If an angler fails to gauge the nibble properly, he or she may lose a fish by either overreacting to a weak nibble or not reacting in time to a strong one.

In fishing and in your love life, gauge your early responses wisely so that you can counter immediately with appropriate, properly measured, and precise actions.

MY TYPICAL FIRST DATE

My first date with an attractive attorney named Nora was at *Damon's Japanese Restaurant*. It's a fun place by the beach with loud rock 'n roll music, lots of sake drinking, and delicious fresh seafood and sushi.

I ordered teriyaki chicken (the cheapest dinner on the menu) while Nora ordered the broiled sea scallops entree (one of the most expensive items on the menu).

> "The traditional male-female dynamics is enjoyable. We like doors opened for us and meals paid for on the first date. Otherwise we think he's cheap."
>
> Christina Hoff Sommers
> *Esquire Magazine*, February 1994

At the end of the meal, I noticed that Nora hadn't finished three of her scallops. It just so happens that I absolutely love to eat scallops. But since it was our first date, I didn't have the nerve to ask her if I could eat her leftovers. I didn't want to come across as being cheap. She also ordered two glasses of chardonnay from the wine list at $7.50 a glass. Luckily for me and my pocketbook, she didn't order a piece of strawberry cheesecake to go.

Dating reveals clues about a person's personality, desires, values, lifestyle, and character. Nora's challenge was to find out whether I regarded her as being worth it or if I was just a plain cheapskate.

Not being worthy is grounds for ending the dating relationship immediately. Being a cheapskate, while not being a very endearing quality, is a far lesser evil.

I've figured out why first dates don't work any better than they do. It's because they take place in restaurants. Women are weird and confused and unhappy about food, and men are weird and confused and unhappy about money, yet off they go, the minute they meet, to where you use money to buy food.

Adair Lara
Author of *Welcome to Earth, Mom* (1992)

GAUGE THE JERKS ON YOUR LINE MORE CAREFULLY

To help you access your early dating "nibbles" more accurately, here are a few items well worth considering:

- ☞ **Don't get faked out early.** Sophia Irene Loeb, author of *Epigrams of Eve,* wrote, "Platonic friendship [is]: The interval between the introduction and the first kiss." It is easy to get faked out by a man's behavior in the early stages of a dating relationship. The man you are trying to gauge accurately and wisely is more clearly revealed over time.

- ☞ **Find enjoyable dating experiences.** Dating is a process of getting to know the other person. You can make the process a lot more fun by having enjoyable dating experiences. It's a great way to get out and enjoy an active lifestyle. Dating naturally reveals tastes, values, character, and lifestyle habits.

- ☞ **Let things unfold slowly.** A hit song from the 1960's was titled, "*You Can't Hurry Love.*" Be patient and let love happen naturally. There's no need to tell your life story on your first date. If your relationship has any future, there will be plenty of time later. Slowing things down also has the side-benefit of letting potential passion build up.

- ☞ **Measure the size of a man's heart.** An English proverb reads, "Measure men around the heart." A good measure of a man is the consistent amount of warmth, kindness, goodness, patience, gratitude, and sincerity he possesses. These qualities are not created instantly. They are emotional habits that are highly valued in a long-term love relationship.

🐟 **Be a critical judge of character.** If you want a relationship to last in quality, be sure you select a man who is honest. It is a trait that may be disguised by words, but revealed by actions. Judge more by what a man does rather than what he says. A good loving relationship is built on a solid foundation of trust. Gain the upper hand in this new relationship by making this crystal clear to him early on.

🐟 **Observe his friends for clues.** A Japanese proverb reads, "When the character of a man is not clear to you, look at his friends." Don't underestimate the power of influence. Observe the habits of a man's friends. Their actions are rarely any different than the one you're dating when his guard is down.

🐟 **Trust your intuition.** Dr. Joyce Brothers, psychologist and syndicated columnist, wrote, "Trust your hunches. Hunches are based on facts filed away just below the conscious level." If you sense that something is wrong, you're probably right. Back off and let time reveal the truth. Realize that there are a lot of sneaky men in the dating world that can be very skilled at fooling innocent women. Make your relationship choices before you get emotionally or physically involved. It's smarter and easier this way.

By following an intelligent approach to dating, you can stay focused on your primary goal of landing a quality man with sincere intentions for consistent long-term happiness.

KEEP YOUR LIFE BALANCED

Dating can be at times either joyful or heartbreaking. But most importantly, it is necessary. Dr. Judy Kuriansky, author of *The Complete Idiot's Guide to Dating*, wrote, "Remember to treat dating as simply getting to know a person better."

Intelligent dating requires good judgment. By maintaining a rich balanced life (physical, mental, emotional, financial, social, family, career, hobbies, contributions, and causes), you will be in a better position to judge which man and situation is right for you and which ones are not.

> "You may be attracted to characteristics in a love partner you later become repelled by."
> Dr. Harold H. Bloomfield
> Author of *Love Secrets for a Lasting Relationship* (1992)

Unlike your high school days, dating is not an end in itself. As a mature adult, dating serves as a means to finding someone well-suited for a passionate, romantic, intimate, fulfilling, and committed love relationship (marriage).

Enjoyable dating is simply a more interesting and exciting way to help you do the sorting.

THE BOTTOM LINE

Men are like fish. They are creatures of habit. Only pick men with emotional, mental, relationship, and lifestyle habits you can live with on a regular basis. Be smart. Watch for clues and get good at gauging the jerks at the end of your line. Avoid getting involved with men who are more likely to bring consistent pain rather than consistent happiness into your life.

Seamed stockings aren't subtle but they certainly do the job. You shouldn't wear them when out with someone you're not prepared to sleep with, since their presence is tantamount to saying, "Hi there, big fellow, please rip my clothes off at your earliest opportunity." If you really want your escort paralytic with lust, stop frequently to adjust the seams.

Cynthia Heimel
Author of *Sex Tips for Girls* (1983)

Seventeen

The Strike

SET YOUR HOOK PROPERLY

There is no second chance with an experienced trout. I might trick a six-inch native trout or even a ten-inch stocked trout, but to catch a veteran trout, twelve inches or more, I must be perfect, and I seldom am.

Le Anne Schreiber
Former editor of *The New York Times* Sports Section
from
The Angler's Book of Daily Inspiration by Kevin Nelson

strike: 1. a sudden hit on an angler's fishing line. 2. when a fish decides to snatch the bait. 3. the defining moment when a man is vulnerable to falling in love with you.

Love can strike in an instant. The trouble is that you never know when, where, who, or especially, if it will happen.

In the movie, *Sleepless in Seattle,* Tom Hanks plays a single parent who struggles with life after his wife's recent passing.

When asked about his love for his late wife, he said, "It was a million tiny things that when you add them all up, it just meant that we were supposed to be together, and I knew it. I knew it the very first time that I touched her. It was like coming home. Only to no home that I'd ever known. I was just taking her hand to help her out of the car, and I knew it. It was like magic."

When a man falls in love, there is a defining moment when he suddenly feels the magic and the power of love for a particular woman. Without such a moment, a man remains uncertain and restless about his romance. But with this magical romantic moment, he instantly becomes emotionally hooked on the woman.

For love to last, a clever woman must cultivate and take full advantage of these rare magical romantic moments.

A SIMPLE FISHING ANALOGY

In the sport of fishing, a strike is when the fish takes a big hit on the bait or lure of the angler. It is usually a sudden and decisive action on the part of the fish.

John M. Cole, author of *Striper: A Story of Fish and Man,* wrote, "The strike is a gift the barracuda keeps for its fisherman and always gives with grace. Even though the fish has been seen, even though impending contact has been announced by the creature itself, the meeting has the jolt of a slap on the shins with a two-by-four, the shock of a kick in the groin. Wham!"

When a fish is about to strike with impact, the angler must take advantage of the situation by using a method called "setting the hook." This is done by pulling back on the fishing rod in order to sink the sharp point of the hook deeply and securely into the jaw of the fish.

> "There is a final moment of unyielding patience which, in angling, so often makes the difference between fish and no fish."
>
> Sparse Grey Hackle
> Author of *Fishless Days, Angling Nights* (1971)

Setting the hook prevents the fish from falling off during the difficult landing process. Many fish are lost because of weak hook-ups caused by improperly setting the hook.

In the sport of fishing and in your love life, be sure to set the hook properly so your prized catch doesn't fall off when you're trying to land him.

AN UNCONSCIOUS PROCESS CALLED ANCHORING

For several years, I enrolled in personal development courses that utilized a therapeutic technique called neurolinguistic programming or NLP. NLP incorporates a light trance hypnosis to rewire the unconscious mind in order to help a person eliminate fears and accomplish goals.

Love can "strike" instantly:
A woman hooks a man
good when his guard is
down and she is at her
feminine best. But a
woman spooks a man away
early when his guard is up
and she's at her worst. A
smart woman realizes that
she must hook him quickly
before there is any chance
of spooking him away. This
clever woman knows that
after a man is smitten with
love he will put up with
almost anything.

Steve Nakamoto
Author of *Men Are Like Fish*

One NLP tool is called anchoring. It is a way of intentionally creating stimulus-response patterns in the brain.

Madison Avenue advertisers spend millions of dollars using these same anchoring techniques. For example, when you see a charismatic social icon like Tiger Woods wearing Nike-brand clothing or driving a new Buick automobile, your brain makes a natural connection between the good feelings you have for Tiger Woods and the products he endorses. The transfer of positive feelings from Tiger Woods to the products he endorses causes people to buy those products.

Anchoring is a way to instantly link the response of powerful emotional feelings to the stimulus of something we see, hear, read, touch, taste, or smell.

> "A man falls in love through his eyes, a woman through her imagination, and then they both speak of it as an affair of 'the heart.'"
> Helen Rowland
> Author of *A Guide to Men* (1922)

In your love life, you want to set the hook by anchoring powerful positive feelings to something unique about you (For example: your smile, name, voice, scent, touch, skin, hair, kiss, laugh, moan, cards, pictures, letters, etc.).

SET YOUR LOVE HOOK PROPERLY

To assist you in anchoring or setting the hook, here are some important points to consider:

- ® **Probe for his emotional hungers.** Dangle your attractive bait or wiggle your feminine lure in a man's most undernourished emotional area. This

is where a man is most vulnerable to you. Find his
starving needs and fill them quickly and elegantly.
Become the consistent source of his happiness and
fulfillment. (For more helpful insight, turn to page
205 and discover "The Seven Emotional Hungers.")

⊗ **Wait patiently for the right moment.** If you act too
early you may frighten the man. If you wait too long
the magic moment may pass. Look for a time of
heightened emotion, when the moment is at its
peak and then make your most daring moves.

⊗ **Don't be afraid to take radical action.** Dave Shiflett,
author of *The Casting Call,* wrote, "When a fish bites
a fake fly, it is much like a person biting into a sand-
wich and discovering a staple. He quickly spits it
out. We must set the hook between the act of biting
and the act of discovery." In order to set the hook
in a man, be sure to offer a massive dose of pure
pleasure before he gets any hint of possible pain. If
he senses the hook early on, he won't strike.

⊗ **Set the hook with the right look.** Men tend to be
visually-oriented, judging from the massive com-
mercial success of *Playboy* and *Penthouse* magazines.
The way you look, dress, groom, posture, and move
your body creates a video in the mind of a man. Be
sure yours is a video worth watching repeatedly.

⊗ **Set the hook with the right sound.** Auditory is the
second most dominant sensory channel. The right
sound means finding the most appealing volume,
pitch, tone, and rhythm in your voice. Like a bad

tune on the radio, if you don't sound appealing a man will turn you off. Make sure your volume and tone controls are set for enjoyable listening.

🐚 **Set the hook with the right touch.** Few things communicate feelings better than the touch of a lover. Whether it's kissing, holding hands, or stroking a man's hair, touch can be magical when it's in the correct location, with the proper amount of pressure, during the peak emotional moment, and with a sensitive man who is caught in the ideal mood.

🐚 **Set the hook with the right words**. American journalist, Marya Mannes, wrote, "All really great lovers are articulate and verbal seduction is the surest road to actual seduction." If you want to cover all the communication bases, don't forget to write or say it in well-chosen, emotionally stirring words.

🐚 **Work on your wiggle**. If bait fishing isn't working, switch to trolling. Flash your alluring qualities by a man, get him to fear a lost opportunity, and watch him bite hard. (Turn to page 164 and learn how to fascinate men with your alluring woman's wiggle.)

Use these ideas to help create your own refined personalized strategies for hooking more deeply and securely into a man's heart and soul.

DON'T TAMPER TOO MUCH WITH THE MAGIC

The methods used by therapists provide insights into a person's behavior. But you must be careful here because the misuse of these methods can easily backfire on you.

A Woman's Alluring Wiggle

When you are faced with a man who won't bite, take a tip from fishing experts: switch from bait fishing to trolling with lures. The secret to trolling is to flash an intriguing lure by a fish (or group of fish) and let the fear of loss cause him to take action or miss out. To help you put more wiggle in your lure and cause men to bite hard now, here are key areas to understand:

THE LURE IN ALLURING: What grabs a man's attention is the seamless, effortless, and unpredictable blending or "wiggle" of 5 attractive feminine character types: the Playmate, the Boss, the Mom, the Pal, and the Saint.

THE PLAYMATE: The flashy side of the lure is called the Playmate. It is the sizzling sexy side of a woman. The common mistake is to neglect showing glimpses of the shiny playmate side to men more often than the other sides.

THE BOSS: Earn a man's respect by showing your competence in a worthwhile area. This does not mean to be a bossy person. It has more to do with demonstrating the leadership qualities to inspire others, take responsibility, define objectives, cut to the chase, and get things done. The feminine boss is especially equipped (more so than the average man) to take charge in an emergency emotional situation.

THE MOM: The one person who understands a man and always claims his innocence to the end is the mom. This does not mean mothering and smothering men. It's more about not passing negative judgment and seeing a man as a more innocent person who can often do or say unwise, unintentional, immature, and inappropriate things (to a reasonable extent).

THE PAL: This side of a woman is the friend who tags along and enjoys the ride of life with her man. The ideal pal is youthful, cheerful, enthusiastic, fun, playful, optimistic, refreshingly innocent, and full of surprises.

THE SAINT: The saint clearly knows and elegantly demonstrates her belief of what is right vs. wrong, safe vs. dangerous, good vs. evil, and kind vs. mean. The saint side of your lure is the moral backbone which is often missing in many men's lives.

FORWARD DIRECTION: The lure of a woman must be going in a genuine forward direction so that she's just passing through a man's life on her way to better things. If a man truly wants her, then he will have to move in the same forward direction or else miss out on her forever.

VARIABLE SPEEDS: A woman must be moving forward in her life at a fast enough pace to cause a man to act, but slow enough at times to allow the man to bite. The fear of loss is one of the most powerful forces in human psychology. Use it wisely to inspire you to progress forward in your life while you are simultaneously getting a man to fully appreciate your unique feminine gifts and to sorely miss your absence in his life.

*The Bottom Line: Work on your wiggle. Make sure that the power of your wiggle significantly exceeds the impact of your early spooking. If you do this right, he won't know what hit him!

A few years ago, I went to the Club Med Village in Cancun, Mexico where I tried my newly-acquired NLP anchoring techniques on unsuspecting female vacationers. Since I was not very adept at performing these techniques, I only accomplished two things: 1) People thought I was a real weirdo, and 2) I jinxed myself out of any possible romance.

> "Not only has one to do one's best, one must,
> while doing one's best, remain detached from
> whatever one is trying to achieve."
> Janwillen Van De Wetering
> Author of *The Empty Mirror* (1999)

At a critical junction, a small shift in your communication style may be the difference between success and failure at getting someone to fall in love with you. For more precise adjustments, consider applying anchoring techniques. Just be sure that you use them sparingly and only when they feel completely natural for you to perform.

When the opportunity at a rare magical romantic moment arrives, be ready to set your hook properly. It is your big chance to secure yourself firmly into the heart and mind of the man you want.

If a man is properly hooked emotionally and physically (in that preferred order), he is much easier to reel in and land safely into your net of commitment and marriage.

THE BOTTOM LINE

You can only expect to land a man who has been properly hooked. Setting the love hook properly requires anticipation, boldness, acute sensitivity, and precise elegant actions.

REAL LIFE ADVENTURES by Gary Wise and Lance Aldrich

A man finally gets married when all the buttons have
fallen off every piece of clothing he owns.

Eighteen

The Landing

PLAY YOUR CATCH INTO THE NET

It's not a fish until it is on the bank.

Irish Proverb
from
The Fisherman's Guide to Life by Criswell Freeman

land•ing: 1. the process of bringing a hooked fish out of the water and either onto land, inside a boat, or into a fishing net. 2. the process of bringing a man out of the uncertain single world and into the safety of a committed loving relationship (marriage). 3. the trickiest part of catching a man.

Some of the most exciting and wonderful romantic relationships can mysteriously fall apart before they reach the commitment or marriage stage.

For example, a few summers ago actress Julia Roberts and her sweetheart, the former star of TV's *Law & Order*, Benjamin Bratt, ended their four-year romance. The front cover of *People Magazine's* July 16, 2001 issue read, "Julia & Ben. WHAT WENT WRONG. Just as friends thought they were headed for the altar, Hollywood's golden couple calls it quits." An intimate said of the pair, "Julia and Ben were deeply in love with each other. It just came to an end."

> "Venus plays tricks on lovers with her game
> of images which never satisfy."
>
> Lucretius
> Roman philosopher and poet (96-55 B.C.)

Romance is a beautiful part of a new relationship. But real love must also pass the tests of time and adversity. After an exciting phase of romance, love must eventually find its way to a secure emotional commitment.

A romance is not love until it rests safely in the landing net of commitment and absolute emotional certainty.

A SIMPLE FISHING ANALOGY

The process of landing a fish is considered one of the most challenging phases in the sport of fishing.

Mike Toth, author of *The Complete Idiot's Guide to Fishing Basics*, wrote, "There are many ways to get a fish out of the water (called "landing" the fish). However, this is when most fish are lost, because, basically, fish do not want to come out of the water. Even tired or 'played out' fish can put forth a burst of energy and try to get away from the angler. Given other factors at this time—a short line, an excited angler, possibly a rocking boat—it's not surprising that many fish succeed in escaping."

> "The end of fishing is not angling, but catching."
> Thomas Fuller
> English author (1608-1661)

In the sport of fishing and in your love life, you must learn how to land your hook-ups effectively. Even the best strikes can be lost to the challenging current of time and adversity.

A SHORT-LIVED LONG-DISTANCE ROMANCE

There was a man named Bill and a woman named Jane who met and fell in love at the Club Med Village in Cancun.

During their week together, they had the time of their lives: swimming in the warm tropical waters, dancing in the disco, taking shopping trips into town, sipping cocktails at sunset, and strolling hand-in-hand on the beach.

I remember seeing the two of them with tears in their eyes as they said good-bye to each other in the Cancun airport at the end of the week long vacation.

There is too little courtship in the world. For courtship means a wish to stand well in the other person's eyes, and, what is more, a readiness to be pleased with the other's ways; a sense on each side of having had the better of the bargain; an under-current of surprise and thankfulness at one's good luck.

Vernon Lee
"In Praise of Courtship,"
Hortus Vitae (1904)

It turns out that Jane was going back to her life as a house-wife with three children and a husband. Bill was going back to the big city and his lifestyle as a single bachelor.

What eventually happened was this: Jane and Bill had another intimate rendezvous. Jane wanted to leave her husband to be with Bill. But Bill was uneasy about having an instant family with three children. Jane separated from her husband. But after a few months, Bill painfully abandoned Jane. Jane was left devastated and disillusioned.

> "Love does not consist in gazing at each other but in looking together in the same direction."
> Antoine De Saint-Exupery
> French author (1900-1944)

In the final analysis, Jane hooked Bill. But she was unable to land him into her net of commitment. There is no denying that the hook-up is the most thrilling part of the "fishing-for-love" process. But without properly landing a romance it remains only a short-lived, pole-bending thrill.

PLAY YOUR PRIZED CATCH INTO THE NET

An Angler's Dictionary by Henry Beard and Roy McKie defines a "net" as a "woven mesh bag attached to a circular wood or metal frame on which a handle is mounted, used to remove hooked fish from the water."

To help you get your romance out of the competitive social waters and into the landing net of commitment (the comfort of absolute emotional certainty that leads directly to engagement and then marriage), here are a few items worth examining more closely:

⑨ **Factor in the current.** The current works in two separate ways. First, the current of good fortune can flow in your direction and make the process of catching too easy. In this case, you have a romance that hasn't tested the strength of your hook-up. Secondly, the current can work against you and make the act of catching extremely difficult. In this case, patience and flexibility will help you withstand adversity. Wisely anticipate abundant amounts of frustration, anger, disappointment, pain, and worry when the current is going against you.

⑨ **Don't let tension break your line.** Just as too much pressure can cause a fishing line to break, too much fighting can break-off a relationship. Understand that upsets are simply when someone violates a standard that you have. If your relationship is to survive, you must learn to understand and appreciate each other. Finding solutions rather than dwelling on problems can be the difference between love or no love. A love ends when your negative convictions reach the point of irreconcilable differences.

⑨ **Play out the fish.** To play in your love relationship means such things as: give and take, tease and be teased, intensity and calm, hot action and cooling off, as well as, togetherness and space. A man isn't ready to settle down and finally commit himself to you until after he's gotten a good share of his thrills out of his system. Let out your line by allowing the man to play himself out. Otherwise he'll fight and resist you all the way in.

☯ **Reset the hooks with the promise of great sex.** Whether you engage in sexual activity or not, the promise of an inspiring sexual future is often times a man's secret primary motivation for continuing the aggressive chase after the woman. But be very careful here. Awkward sex in the beginning can bring an immediate end to your future plans. On the other hand, the images of a great sexual tomorrow can move a man's emotional mountains.

☯ **Remember to reel him in.** In reasonable time and after a man has been fully played out, it's time to reel him in. How much time that is depends on your own situation. But when there's no more to be explored as a dating couple, it's time to move forward in your relationship and your life. Sometimes the most wonderful romances can go no further. Eventually there comes a time when a smart woman either reels him in or cuts him loose.

☯ **Ease him into the net.** Mother Teresa said, "Joy is a net of love by which you can catch souls." You may have to withstand a man's last-minute surge to escape to freedom. This can best be handled with calm assurances rather than demanding pressure. Make commitment easy by painting the future with happiness, contentment, intimacy, joy, comfort, harmony, and, most of all, peace of mind.

Follow these guidelines for developing your own plan of action and you will have an excellent chance of landing even the most challenging and elusive desirable men.

A good woman
inspires a man.

A brilliant woman
interests him.

A beautiful woman
fascinates him.

A sympathetic woman
gets him.

Helen Rowland
Author of *A Guide to Men* (1922)

CREATE A SIMPLY IRRESISTIBLE LOVE FUTURE

William Shakespeare, the 16th century English playwright, wrote, "The trout must be caught with tickling."

In a similar way, a man is not caught by external force; he is captured by internal emotional persuasion.

Some of the most attractive, fascinating, and honorable men can be very difficult to catch because of their mistakes from the past, belief that someone better still awaits them, or lack of understanding about how great relationships (successful marriages) get better, not worse over time.

The only women who can catch these game creatures are those who: 1) thoroughly understand the "men are like fish" principles, 2) display both unyielding patience and unstoppable persistence, 3) act with boldness and precision at the most opportune moments, and 4) possess the enlightened spirit to guide a man through his unfounded fears and into the safety of a more fulfilling and rewarding life together.

As it's been stated throughout this book, preparation, not luck, is the ultimate secret to landing the love you want. Remember that while guys may clamor for sex, it's love that mature men desire and need. Enlightened women use this understanding to catch and keep the romantic whoppers.

THE BOTTOM LINE

Men are like fish. A man is not caught until he is actually landed safely in the net of emotional, rather than verbal commitment. Play your man out and expect a good fight on the way in. Just like a trout, a man must be caught with internal tickling (emotional persuasion), not external force.

Nineteen

Catch & Release

DON'T KILL THE ROMANCE

A good game fish is too valuable
to be caught only once.

Lee Wulff
Author of *Trout on a Fly* (1990)

catch & re•lease: 1. a common practice in the sport of fly-fishing, where the angler sets free a fish unharmed immediately after capture. 2. giving a man enough space to periodically revive himself emotionally so he can continue pursuing a woman he desires. 3. the secret to keeping romance alive.

An age-old French proverb reads, "Love makes time pass; time makes love pass."

We all want a great love life that is exciting, passionate, inspiring, intimate, fulfilling, and lasting. But in today's complex world, this ideal combination is hard to find.

> "The secret of staying in love is learning
> how to make love all the time."
> Barbara DeAngelis, Ph.D.
> Author of *Real Moments for Lovers* (1995)

If we truly want happiness out of our love lives, we must seek and enjoy the thrills of romance while nurturing what it takes to make love grow and last.

MY IRREGULAR FLOWER SHOP CUSTOMERS

For over a decade, I worked in my family's flower shop business. Some of our best customers were the men who were actively dating. These fellows would typically come in once a week to buy a dozen long-stem red roses for their sweethearts. In time, some of these couples would put in a big order with us for their wedding. But after the wedding, many of these previously romantic men would disappear.

The only time we would see them again was on Valentine's Day or if they were in the proverbial doghouse. If they ever returned to our shop as regulars, it would be because they were either divorced or separated and actively dating again. It was a sad, but often true commentary on how the romance in a love relationship tends to fade away over time.

> "It is absurd to say that a man can't love
> one woman all the time as it is to say
> that a violinist needs several violins
> to play the same piece of music."
>> Honore de Balzac
>> French author (1799-1850)

The big romance that stays exciting, grows, and lasts is more the exception than the norm for many people today.

Why that is so remains largely a mystery.

A SIMPLE FISHING ANALOGY

In the sport of fishing, there is a term that is commonly used called "catch and release." This involves removing the hook from the mouth of the fish and letting it swim away to freedom. Sometimes after a bitter struggle, a fish has to be revived before it can be safely released.

According to the *USA Today* February 17, 1999 edition, "Catch and release [is] catching on.... A recent survey said 58% of all anglers practice the catch-and-release fishing method to preserve fish for future generations."

Sheridan Anderson, author of *The Curtis Creek Manifesto,* wrote, "Releasing: Hold gently until the fish can swim away. Don't injure when landing. Catch and release is the only way to insure the quality of the sport."

U.S. DIVORCE STATISTICS
(Source: National Center for Health Statistics)

"Divorce is one of the loneliest of modern rituals. Before, during, and after the actual culmination of the legal process it is an ordeal that rips people away from their roots, their important relationships, and a part of themselves. There is really nothing like it--- except perhaps war."
Susan Gordon, author of *Lonely in America* (1976)

* Current percentage of divorced adults (1998) — 9.8%
* Percentage of first marriages that end in divorce (1997) — 50%
* Percentage of remarriages that end in divorce (1997) — 60%
* Estimated average cost of divorce (1997) — $15,000
* Median duration of marriage (1997) — 7.2 years
* Estimated average length of divorce proceedings (1997) — 1 year
* Percentage of households occupied by one adult person (1997) — 26%
* Adults between 25 and 34 years old never married (1998) — 35%
* Percentage of all householders who are unmarried (2000) — 48%
* Percentage of elderly widows living alone (1998) — 70%
* Median age at first marriage in 1998 for males — 26.7
* Median age at first marriage in 1998 for females — 25
* Median age at divorce in 1998 for males — 35.6
* Median age at divorce in 1998 for females — 33.2
* Average age of males divorcing from their second marriage — 42
* Average age of females divorcing from their second marriage — 39
* State with the lowest divorce rate: Massachusetts (1997) — 2.4%
* State with the highest divorce rate: Nevada (1997) — 9.0%
* Drop in standard of living of females after divorce (2000) — 45%

THE BOTTOM LINE
If left to chance, your love life may end up as just another statistic.
Failing to plan means about the same as planning to fail.

A fish that has been caught and released carefully is available to be fished for again.

In the sport of fishing and in your love life, the art and spirit of "catch & release" is the secret to keeping what you treasure alive and well for the future.

IF YOU LOVE SOMEBODY SET THEM FREE

If it is life-long romance that you desire, don't kill it off early by locking it away like one of your prized possessions. Keep a healthy feeling of freedom in your relationship and let the man chase after your love over and over again.

To prevent your romance from coming to an emotional dead end, here are some ideas to help keep your love relationship vibrant and healthy:

- **Stay attractive.** One of the main reasons why men fade away is that they lose their physical attraction for their mate. Don't neglect this simple reality.

- **Don't mother your mate.** While it may seem natural to mother someone you love, nagging and scolding a man is one of the quickest ways to kill the passion. Stop mothering men and you will be treated more like a woman and he'll feel more like a man.

- **Create space in your relationship.** An English proverb reads, "Familiarity breeds contempt." Maintain some safe breathing room by preserving some of your personal identity, personal interests, and personal friends. Learn to nourish the specialness of your individuality while you simultaneously maintain the connection in your love partnership.

⑨ **Never break the trust.** A Swedish proverb reads, "What a moment broke may take years to mend." Don't break the trust in a relationship by being careless in the moment. Once trust is broken it can never return to its original pristine condition. Keep your romance alive by not crossing the line of trust.

⑨ **Manage your upsets.** Take full responsibility for your own reactions to what others say or do. Realize that a man will only cherish you in direct proportion to how well he is understood and appreciated. Choose to remain unperturbed by the painful but unintentional actions of others. (Turn to page 206 for "Anger Management For Anglers.)

⑨ **Repair with forgiveness.** The only way to fix the past is through complete forgiveness. A French proverb reads, "To understand is to forgive." If someone does something wrong unintentionally or unwisely, the only thing you can do to save your relationship is to be understanding and choose to forgive.

⑨ **Create and develop new channels for growth.** Like a healthy plant, a love relationship is either growing or dying. There are no in-betweens. Keep your romance alive by discovering new ways of enjoying the wonders of an abundant life together.

⑨ **Treasure your moments now!** There may come a time in your life when all you have are your memories. Avoid taking your love for granted. Show your gratitude by valuing it richly now. Don't wait until you lose it in order to appreciate it.

Keeping a romance alive and well is no easy task. By following these simple guidelines and staying committed to nurturing your love relationship, you will be able to handle most problems in advance.

REMEMBER TO KEEP THE MAN CHASING

There's an old saying that goes, "A man quits running after he's caught the bus." For a man to stay romantic, an enlightened woman knows that a small dose of uncertainty keeps a man running after her bus.

A man is emotionally wired to pursue and achieve. Don't try to take that basic instinct away from him. If you do, he may either die romantically or chase after another woman.

> "Pursuit and seduction are the essence of sexuality. It's part of the sizzle."
> Camille Paglia
> Author of *Sex, Art, and American Culture* (1992)

A Spanish proverb reads, "Take hold lightly; let go lightly. This is one of the great secrets of felicity in love."

A keeper in a love relationship is not someone you hold as a possession to lock up and throw away the key. Instead, a keeper is the one that you let go of lightly but keeps coming back to you naturally for more and more.

THE BOTTOM LINE

Men are like fish. If you catch and cage them, the game in their hearts dies. But if you release them and keep them emotionally/passionately alive, they are free to revive themselves and resume the love chase they so instinctively desire.

There is a love that begins
in the head, and goes down
to the heart, and grows
slowly; but it lasts till death,
and asks less than it gives.
There is another love, that
blots out wisdom, that is
sweet with the sweetness
of life and bitter with the
bitterness of death, lasting
for an hour; but it is worth
having lived a whole life
for that hour.

Ralph Iron
Author of *The Story of an African Farm* (1883)

Twenty

The Keeper

ENJOY THE JOURNEY

When I have made a difficult cast and
landed it the way I wanted, or fished
over a difficult fish and finally
caught it, I feel true reward.

Jennifer Smith
Author of *Paul Bunyan*:
My Wooly Bugger Chuckling Machine
from
The Angler's Book of Daily Inspiration by Kevin Nelson

keep•er: 1. a big fish worth taking home with pride. 2. a man who contributes massive, consistent, and secure happiness to your life. 3. the love every woman cherishes and needs.

Here are the final words of the last song ever recorded by the greatest musical group of all-time (according to the 1998 VH1 Poll of Musical Artists), the Beatles, from a song appropriately titled, "The End":

> And in the end...
> The love you take
> Is equal to the love...
> You make.

An enlightened woman never leaves her love life entirely to luck. Instead, she wisely chooses the path of physical, mental, and emotional preparation.

As a final checklist for making love happen in your life, always remember to:

- ⍟ Start with a fresh positive attitude
- ⍟ Maximize your physical talents
- ⍟ Develop more emotional heart and character
- ⍟ Play the percentages in your favor
- ⍟ Seek honest, objective feedback
- ⍟ Make accurate adjustments in your actions
- ⍟ Stay centered and refuse to give up

Naturally, there are some women who might be inclined to say something like, "Men hardly seem worth the trouble. I can live happily without them. Why should I go through all the relationship hassles again?"

After all, Gloria Steinem, the noted American feminist (who got married in 2000) and author, once said, "A woman without a man is like a fish without a bicycle."

My best reply is that love preparation is not only about getting a man. Love preparation has a lot to do with learning about people and participating fully in the adventure of life.

ENJOY YOUR NEVER-ENDING LOVE JOURNEY

The final message of this book is:

> Love is a journey, not a destination.
> So most of all, enjoy the journey.

Getting the love you want is only the frosting on the cake. Becoming the special kind of soul who deserves love by giving away love is a far greater and lasting value.

> "Love is never lost. If not reciprocated, it will
> flow back and soften and purify the heart."
> Washington Irving
> American essayist (1783-1859)

When you come to the end of your life, there will be more to treasure than your collection of old photographs and love letters. You will also possess the eternal heart and the sparkle in your eyes of a truly loving human being.

THE LOVE KEEPER TEST

A love relationship with a man is a keeper if you can say "yes" to all five of these:

1) It feels right.

2) It's in my best interests.

3) It's in his best interests.

4) It serves a greater good.

5) The heavens are smiling.

Steve Nakamoto
Author of *Men Are Like Fish*

A popular saying goes, "You can't take it with you." No words are more true when it comes to the endless acquiring of material possessions. But the one thing that you can take with you, however, is love.

LOVE IS THE KEEPER

Elbert G. Hubbard, the American author (1856-1915), wrote, "The love you give away is the only love we keep."

Unlike fishing for fish, there are very few "keepers" in life. One of those, however, is love. It is a treasure for eternity, not to be missed for any reason.

Over the course of a person's entire life there are no real excuses for missing out on love, except for the false illusions of fear and self-doubt. It is my hope that this book has done a lot to reduce or eliminate these destructive illusions entirely from your life.

> "What we have once enjoyed we can never lose.
> All that we love deeply becomes a part of us."
> Helen Keller
> American lecturer (1880-1968)

You now possess all you need to catch the big romance and bring it home for keeps. If you get on and stay on the path of love mastery as I have presented in this book, there's nothing really stopping you from becoming simply irresistible and acquiring the happiness and joy you rightfully deserve.

Please go out and make love happen....now!

We, the fish, are getting tired of swimming around aimlessly. Our natural destiny is to be caught by your true love.

Good luck and God bless.

Permissions

About the Author

Steve Nakamoto is a former human relations/communications instructor for Dale Carnegie & Associates and personal development trainer for world renowned motivation and peak performance expert Tony Robbins.

Steve has spent the last few years as an international tour director taking clients on first-class vacation trips. With more than 150 cruises, Club Med vacations, Singles' Ski Weeks, and escorted vacation tours, Steve has had a lot of first-hand experience learning about men and women of all ages, backgrounds, and cultures.

His earlier experience managing his family's retail florist businesses along with the Nakamoto family's annual trout fishing vacations has helped shape Steve's unique "fishy" perspective on how to "land" romantic love.

The first edition of *Men Are Like Fish* received honorable mention recognition in the *Writer's Digest 2000 Self-Published Non-Fiction Book Awards.* That edition went on to sell foreign language translation rights to Spain, Japan, Israel, Taiwan, Korea, Thailand, Russia, and the Czech Republic.

Steve has appeared on over 200 radio and television talk shows including *NBC's "The Other Half"* starring Dick Clark, Mario Lopez, and Danny Bonaduce. He currently serves as the featured dating/relationship expert on iVillage.com's popular "Ask Mr. Answer Man" discussion board.

Uncanny Advice For Fish (Men)

> "Men don't live well by themselves. They don't even
> live like people. They live like bears with furniture."
> —Rita Rudner, American comedian

Men Are Like Fish is written primarily for women, but there are many ideas in the book that would be useful to enlighten men with as well. Here are a few insights that are designed to help men dramatically improve their love lives:

BECOME A BIG FISH: The path of self-improvement also applies to men. A smart man does all he can to become the kind of man that a woman truly wants. That means a man should: get a fresh start, maximize his talents, develop his game, play with more heart, and move up in class. Don't get "thrown back" for not measuring up to a sensitive, intelligent woman's standards.

RISE TO THE SURFACE: A smart man makes himself available to the right kind of women, in the right types of places, and at the most appropriate times. If a man wants to be discovered and appreciated, then he must get himself in a good position to be caught. Don't get old and lazy by living your life at the bottom of the lake (with other socially lazy fish) in the safety of obscurity.

MAKE A BIG SPLASH: When you are in the presence of prospective women, do something bold that draws attention to your ability to take action without fear. Women dig a big fish with lots of game. If the situation is appropriate, give them a sample of what you are made of and stand out from the crowd.

DON'T BE AFRAID TO BITE: When a man is presented with the bait of true love from a desirable woman who is an excellent fit, then it's important to act boldly while the opportunity is there. A sensible woman soon tires of a man who is afraid to make any strong moves in her direction. Don't let some small fry sneak in and steal your chances with her. Examine her bait and if you like it...act fast & bite hard! Remember that true love always gets better with time.

MAKE HER POLE BEND: Once a man decides to bite, make sure to thrill her with passion, fun, intimacy, and romance. A smart man never has his game minimized by emotional fear. Love is supposed to be an example of life being lived at its fullest. Give her lots of thrilling action. Don't disappoint her by being a romantic dead weight.

DON'T DIE: It's your responsibility to revive yourself emotionally especially after being caught by love. Stay alive, passionate, fun, and romantic. Be thankful for the woman in your life. If you stay alive, so will love.

GET HUNGRY NOW!: French moralist, Jean de La Bruyere (1645-1696) warned all men when he said, "A bachelor's life is a fine breakfast, a flat lunch, and a miserable dinner." Never take your love life for granted. One day, the gap may be too large between what you want and what you can attain. Let somebody love you before it's too late. Nobody wants to catch a tired old fish.

*A Note to Women: The better you understand a man, the more deeply he feels appreciated, and the more often you will be cherished in return.

Notes on the Bait Self-Quiz

"Men love and fall in love romantically,
women sensibly and rationally."
—Nancy Chodorow, sociologist
from *Men: Quotations About Men By Women* (1993)

The Bait Self-Quiz (on page 80) was designed to give women a handy tool for understanding the power of their attraction with men. Here are some observations that should be taken into account when you're taking the test:

BE OUTSTANDING AT SOMETHING: On the quiz, the highest grade you can give yourself is "excellent." But there is another higher rating called "outstanding" which leaves a lasting impression on men. While only a few are blessed with being "outstanding" in talent, anyone can develop "outstanding" traits in game, heart and character. In a competitive environment with plenty of choices, men are only impacted by the "outstanding" traits of women.

DON'T BE POOR IN ANYWAY: On the other hand, men can be negatively impacted by a single "poor" rating in any category. The game of love is won by playing into your strengths and handling your weaknesses. Be sure to take care of any glaring weaknesses, especially early on.

TALENT AND GAME NATURALLY COME FIRST: I've been asked whether there is any significance to the order of the quiz and the answer is "yes." The things that are noticed initially are talent (appearance) and game (personality). You only get one chance at a first impression, so make sure that you start here. "Heart" and "Character" may in fact be much more important over the long run, but they are more "time-released" in nature.

PLAY YOUR FEMININE CARD: Dr. Toni Grant, a renowned talk-show psychologist, says it's the feminine side of women that men find most alluring. So if you want a man as a lover rather than a friend or business associate, you must cleverly bring your femininity to the forefront with prospective men. If your nature is to be more masculine, then there's nothing wrong with aiming for the "strong and silent" type.

BE ATTRACTIVE IN A MAN'S EYES: To attract men as lovers, be sure to appeal to their tastes rather than to that of other women. Your women friends may mislead you into thinking that you're done working on your talents and game. But an enlightened woman gauges her attraction powers by the actual response of men who seek women as mates.

DON'T BAIT AND SWITCH: Remember to stay attractive and never let negatives build up. In sports, coaches often say that their strategy for success in the playoff rounds is to "go with what got them there in the first place." Maintain your physical attractiveness, magnetic personality, unshakable character, and warm receptive heart. Do it not only for the man you love but, more importantly, for yourself.

*The Bottom Line: To attract attractive people you must first be attractive. Remember that quality men checkout the most attractive bait first.

194

A Word About the Big Fish Test

Here are a few additional comments that I have regarding the Big Fish Test (featured on page 108) which should greatly increase its value to you:

LOOK OUT FOR GLARING WEAKNESSES: The test will often times expose glaring weaknesses in your relationship with a particular man. Low scores in any area should be evaluated closely. While no person or situation is totally perfect, you have to ask yourself if you can tolerate such deficiencies. If true love and long-term happiness are your dream, is this weakness really okay?

UNDERSTAND THE POWER OF "OUTSTANDING": I purposely made the test simpler by removing a category beyond "excellent" called "outstanding." The reason I did so was because outstanding features in either talent or game can blind a woman from a man's key emotional and character flaws. On the other hand, outstanding scores for heart and character should be appreciated more greatly. Be especially cautious of a man with extraordinary talent or game, and be more appreciative of outstanding heart and character.

DON'T MISTAKE COCKINESS FOR CONFIDENCE: A cocky guy puts down others and uses anger to make himself feel superior to others. A confident guy is secure about his own worth to himself and others. One is a builder, while the other is a wrecker. They may look the same on the outside, but they are completely different on the inside. Go for the guy with true self-confidence because cockiness will eventually turn its ugly focus on you.

FOCUS ON A MAN'S HABITS: Like a great magician who fools the audience by controlling the focus on the wrong object, a man can often disguise his true self in the short-term. What a man says may be far different than what he actually does. Habits are your best indicator for sizing up character.

SEPARATE THE MEN FROM THE BOYS: Often times the men who score the highest in the "game" category, are the very ones who are also the most immature. This is particularly tricky for women because it takes a mature man to appreciate that the fire of initial romance is joyfully replaced by the warmth of intimacy, comfort, and family. Be careful of the boys who are in search of endless romantic or sexual "highs." Save your heart for the ones who are at least making the mature transition from boys to men.

GET A RELIABLE SECOND OPINION: For added perspective have a trusted friend or family member take the same test regarding your situation. They may shed additional light on you and your relationship both positive and negative. Just ask them to evaluate objectively with your best interests in mind.

DO THE RIGHT THING: If the relationship you're in feels so right, is it possible for it to be wrong? The answer is "yes." Weigh emotions and truth on separate scales because it is easy to be sincerely wrong. The best policy is to only act if these four conditions are met: 1) It's good for you, 2) It's good for the other person, 3) It's the right thing to do, and 4) It feels right to you. Make more intelligent evaluations and always do the right thing.

***The Bottom Line: Decisions determine your love destiny.
Make smart evaluations and remember that it only takes one.**

Internet Dating Strategies

"If you attract women, men will follow."
—Cindy Hennessy
President of Match.com

The latest craze in the dating game is popularly called cyberdating. And while the online dating business is booming in numbers, it still presents a lot of new challenges in the quest for ultimately finding true love. Here are some observations I've made recently in this dynamic field that might help you along:

IT'S LIKE BUYING SOMETHING "SIGHT, UNSEEN": Don't be fooled by the words that come across your computer screen. Real human interaction is done face-to-face with your eyes and ears. Don't get carried away with your computer. Digital data alone does not make a legitimate first impression. Think of online dating as only an introduction. Try to talk on the phone and meet in person as soon as possible. Don't develop emotionally attachments to people you haven't even met yet.

PEOPLE NOTORIOUSLY MISREPRESENT: Behind a computer terminal a person can be beautiful, unmarried, successful, and all together wonderful, but their reality could be a lot different. Beware of old photos and lots of exaggerations. Ask for honesty up front and even then proceed cautiously. For your part, be sure to take a great photo and have someone else write a good copy ad for you. Also, make sure that you use a "paying," not "free" site. You will avoid most underage or married players that way.

CYBERDATING TAKES UP TIME: It may be flattering at first to receive a lot of responses to your ads like you've suddenly become a far more interesting person overnight. But the reality is that Internet dating is an easy way to make a bold pass at lots of people. Limit your parameters or else this will be a chore.

IT'S A BACKWARDS WAY TO DATE: Cyberdating causes people to sort through others quickly as if it were a job interview. Asking too many questions up front is not how romances naturally begin. Use the Internet as a convenient way to make a quick connection. After that try to return to square one where you get to know someone slowly and see if you like each other.

EVERYONE'S GUARD IS UP AND RIGHTFULLY SO: Internet dating is easy to enter and there is no way of checking the facts. The smart thing is to proceed cautiously remembering that there are a lot of sneaky men out there who are skilled at fooling innocent women. Trust your instincts.

MANY WILL TRY, BUT FEW WILL STAY: Because it can be tiresome and awkward in nature, many will give it up shortly. Therefore, be on the lookout for those who are new to the program. They are less likely to be weird, desperate, or jaded. Shy away from those who have a long cyberdating history.

*The Bottom Line: Take an enlightened approach to cyberdating. While it may increase your numbers, it still may not get you any closer to love. But if you must, try it out with caution and realistic expectations. Maybe you'll get lucky and meet someone passing through who is either simple or enlightened.

Your Best Fishing Buddies

"Friends are the family we choose for ourselves."
—Comtesse Diane
Author of *Les Glanes de la Vie* (1898)

Jim Rohn, author of *Seven Habits for Wealth and Happiness*, wrote, "Keep the weeds of negative influence from your life. Instead farm the seeds of constructive influence. You will not believe the harvest of good fortune you will reap." To help you select good friends (male and female) to go fishing for love with, here are some important things to look for:

BUDDIES WHO MOTIVATE YOU: Get around the type of people whose energy, enthusiasm, and optimism rubs off on you. Avoid negative people who drain your emotions. The best fishing buddies are those who love the sport and can't wait to try out new things and accept the challenges. Let their confidences become yours. And let their playful spirit keep you loose.

BUDDIES WHO SHARE THE SUGAR: Good friends don't hog all the glory or try to get the attention of all the guys. You want friends who understand that the success of the group depends on involving everyone. A good friend is on the lookout for ideal matchups. But for the matchups to work each person in the group must be able to shine. Associate with those who make room for you to share your special gifts with others.

BUDDIES WHO SELL YOU: One of the best ways to convey the essence of your individual strengths is to have friends tell others when you are not present. Great buddies love to share their endorsements of you while claiming ignorance about any of your weaknesses. They can share their positive convictions about you where your natural inclinations of modesty will not.

BUDDIES WHO TAKE YOU PLACES: You can rapidly expand your number of social fishing holes by having your buddies take you places that you would ordinarily find uncomfortable. Going to new places is like taking a fishing trip. A good group of friends can make this a fun adventure and take you to out-of-the-way places where the big ones have their guard down.

BUDDIES WHO PROTECT YOU: Competition among women for the favorable attention of men is commonplace. While it's helpful to be able to stand your ground against unfriendly attacks from rivals, a good friend can save you the hassle and defend your backside. Sometimes the most damaging attacks come from an unexpected direction.

BUDDIES WHO RAISE YOUR STANDARDS: Great buddies maintain your ideals of the person you truly are. They won't allow you to tear yourself down. True friends keeps your head up and your eyes pointed forward. They know that your purpose in life is to be all you can be so that you can get the good that you deserve. True friends hold you to a higher personal standard.

*The Bottom Line: Don't underestimate the power of influence.
If you associate with a great crowd, you'll have more fun with the sport
and enjoy greater success while you're fishing for love.

When A Bachelor Gets Spooked

"If you never want to see a man again, say,
'I love you, I want to marry you, I want to
have children'—they leave skid marks."
—Rita Rudner, comedian
in The New York Times (1985)

There's an old saying in the sport of fishing that goes, "frightened fish can't be caught." The same is also true in romantic love relationships. But when it comes to spooked bachelors, the blame should be equally shared. Sometimes it's the man who is unenlightened and can't appreciate a woman's genuine worth. Other times it's the woman who inadvertently repels rather than attracts men (either physically, emotionally, or spiritually).

Please brace yourself for this honest, but politically incorrect list of things that may spook men away early. Smart women will give love a fair chance by doing their best to keep these "spooking" items to a minimum especially in the early stages. Keep in mind that almost all of these items have little or no effect after a man is smitten with love. (Hint: Set the hook early!)

Most importantly, don't let this touchy subject upset you too much (Rule #1: Angry anglers catch no fish!). Instead, let the general information guide you in the direction of more positive actions and better results in your love life.

BACHELOR HANG-UPS: WHEN HE HAS BIG LOVE OBSTACLES

* Physical Mismatches: When a small man meets a big woman
* Geographically Undesirable: When she lives too far away
* The Age Factor: When she's out of his desired dating range
* The Non-Feminine Woman: When she's too manly for his tastes
* Getting Jobbed: When her choice of occupation annoys him too much
* High-Powered Women: When he gets too easily intimidated by her

THE 5 SENSES: WHEN SHE GETS AN INSTANT REJECTION

* Be a heavy smoker, drinker, or drug user
* Wear too much make-up or have heavily blemished skin
* Have an unappealing perfume to him (or wear too much)
* Be poorly groomed or wear unflattering/inappropriate attire
* Have poor hygiene, bad breath, or unpleasant body odor
* Look unhealthy, unfit, or have low energy
* Have poor standing, walking, or sitting posture
* Frown too much or don't smile enough naturally

198

NON-RAPPORT: WHEN THE CONFLICT IS UNCONSCIOUS

* Have an unpleasant sounding voice
* Speak with a strong foreign accent or heavy twang
* Speak too fast, too slow, or too loud
* Make someone uncomfortable with too much or too little eye contact
* Have absolutely nothing in common with the other person
* Stand too close or too far away from someone while they're talking

CONFIDENCE LEVEL: WHEN HER BIGGEST ENEMY IS WITHIN

* Be painfully shy, fearful, quiet, or deeply depressed
* Have suicidal or "fatal attraction" tendencies
* Lack any natural enthusiasm or be too negative
* Be too sensitive to harmless remarks or the slightest criticism
* Put yourself down too much or not take a compliment very well

PERSONALITY QUIRKS: WHEN SHE SEEMS A LITTLE STRANGE

* Have a weird sense of humor or laugh at the wrong time
* Wear bizarre clothes or have strange personal tastes
* Be too hyper, antsy, or emotionally high-strung
* Stare at people too long or have a strange laugh
* Make too many dramatic facial expressions
* Be a big fan of the occult or a strange religion or be part of a cult
* Be too much of a character or have an unflattering nickname
* Have strange, gross, or unhealthy eating and drinking habits

SMALL TALK: WHEN WHAT SHE SAYS WORKS AGAINST HER

* Gossip excessively about trivial matters
* Use baby talk excessively in the effort to sound cute
* Be highly opinionated or voice a strong prejudice
* Say gross or distasteful things like "I've got diarrhea"
* Express with wild hand gestures
* Ask too many questions that make him feel uncomfortable
* Consistently bring up unpleasant topics
* Jump to conclusions especially negative ones or be a know-it-all
* Insist on telling long uninterrupted personal stories
* Have an annoying pet phrase like "been there done that"

AUDIENCE RATING: WHEN SHE'S A POOR LISTENER
* Finish his sentences or correct his grammar
* Spend far more time talking than listening
* Frequently interrupt while other people are speaking
* Don't give any kind of positive feedback to the talker
* Make the focus of conversations about you and your interests
* Give immediate unsolicited advice often
* Insist on slower speakers to speed it up

EMOTIONAL BAGGAGE: WHEN SHE BRINGS HIM DOWN
* Be sarcastic, cynical, condescending or be a smart-ass
* Create an emotional scene or have a violent temper
* Be too judgmental about innocent male behaviors
* Always seem to take the position of being the victim
* Keep bringing up past hurts from other men
* Criticize, condemn, or complain excessively

CHARACTER FLAWS: WHEN SHE DOES THE WRONG THING
* Be caught or condone blatant lying, stealing, or cheating
* Sleep around with lots of men (usually more than one)
* Engage in regular activities that are illegal or morally wrong
* Intentionally hurt or be mean to other people
* Fail to recognize the necessity for responsibility and duty
* Have a bad reputation of being too promiscuous
* Date married men and think that there is nothing wrong with it

PEOPLE PROBLEMS: WHEN OTHERS SPOIL THE MAGIC
* Have friends who reveal unflattering details about you
* Have him know that you report all your dating detail to your friends
* Have no friends and appear lonely
* Run around with a weird or dangerous crowd
* Clash with a guy's best friends or close family members
* Have no privacy and always be surrounded by others
* Get into nasty public cat fights that bring out the worst in you
* Have friends who cut in on your best love prospects
* Reveal that you have a violent and jealous ex-lover

THE MISSING PLAYMATE: WHEN THE CHEMISTRY ISN'T THERE

* Be too much of a comedian and never resist a punch line
* Be too aggressive about pursuing men
* Be too much of a control freak and be in charge of everything
* Always take the position of a saint
* Be too mothering toward a man that you date
* Lack youthfulness, innocence, fun, and/or playfulness
* Be clueless about how to be sexy or feminine

LIFESTYLE CLASH: WHEN THE FUTURE LOOKS LIKE A HASSLE

* Own too many pets especially cats crawling around your place
* Have obnoxious or out-of-control kids living with you
* Live like a slob or live in a dump
* Be a hard-core feminist, political activist, or hard-core anything
* Be totally insensitive to his love for sports
* Have excessive "girlie" tastes in your home decor
* Have race or religion issues that look like major future conflict
* Have a major class or cultural difference
* Have completely different eating, sleeping, or living habits
* Design plans for vacations and holidays that don't match well

CASH CRUNCH: WHEN HER NEEDS APPEAR TOO COSTLY

* Refer often to your biological clock ticking away
* Own too many credit cards and come across as a big shopper
* Talk about the dream house and lifestyle that he could never afford
* Have a reputation for being flaky especially in finance and career
* Live in a bad part of town or drive an old clunker
* Have a bad job or lack vocational competence or be unemployed

DINNER FOR TWO: WHEN THERE'S A RESTAURANT PROBLEM

* Be rude to waiters and waitresses
* Eat like a horse or display poor table manners
* Always order the most expensive items on the menu
* Get sloppy drunk or throw up while you're on a date
* Order fine wines or dessert when the man appears thrifty
* Be an extremely picky eater and appear too hard to please

DATING MISCUES: WHEN SHE DOESN'T PASS THE AUDITION
* Dress and act inappropriately for a big public or social occasion
* Be a terrible dancer and insist on dancing
* Create an embarrassing emotional scene in public
* Flirt with other men when you're on a date
* Talk too long to people on your cell phone when out on a date
* Forget to say "thank you" or show gratitude in any way
* Point out all the cute guys you see while out on a date

AWKWARD SEX: WHEN HE FREAKS OUT IN THE FRENZY
* Be a bad kisser or be too bold about kissing early
* Have poor hygiene or be unclean when the moment arrives
* Surprise him with uncomfortable or untimely kinkiness
* Do a very poor job of talking dirty in the effort to turn him on
* Be too wild, too bold, or too loud when he's definitely not there yet
* Blurt out freaky things while you're in the frenzy

LOVE PRESSURE: WHEN THINGS HAPPEN TOO FAST FOR HIM
* Leave lots of personal things at his place
* Call him pet names like "sweetie" or "honey" too early on
* Shower him with gifts before he gives you anything
* Send him cards with strong feelings revealed early
* Call him frequently and leave long messages
* Ask for constant reassurances about his feelings for you
* Refer to him as your boyfriend when it's only date #2 or #3
* Talk like you're a couple and make too many plans for the future
* Like him significantly more than he likes you early on
* Insist on meeting his family rather than letting him initiate
* Say "I love you" before that thought ever occurs to him

MARRIAGE PHOBIA: WHEN COMMITMENT TRIGGERS PANIC
* Insist on moving in and living together early on
* Talk about having a huge, expensive, or formal wedding
* Talk about quitting your job and becoming a full-time housewife
* After the engagement bring out a load of undisclosed problems
* After the engagement reveal a radical new set of rules for him

Notes on Spooking Away Men

"Men are subconsciously afraid of women."
—Nellie McClung, Canadian writer
from *Men: Quotations About Men By Women* (1993)

In doing radio interviews across the country, nothing stirs up more controversy with men and women than my takes on "spooking." To help clarify the extreme value of this unique "fishing for love" perceptional tool, I've put together what I consider the most important points to remember for your use.

FRIGHTENED FISH (MEN) CAN'T BE CAUGHT: The slightest hint of a negative vibration and the fish is spooked away. Repeated attempts to hook a spooked fish or man are completely useless. Only a significant space of time and a new type of bait will have any effect on that particular creature.

SPOOKING USUALLY PRECEDES HOOKING: Spooking a man happens in the first moments of encounter. When you are meeting or dating men, their guard is almost always up although they can be very clever in disguising their caution. Your first steps are to put him at ease and to make sure that you're not being evaluated at your less-than-best.

YOU SPOOK HIM WHEN HIS GUARD IS UP: The way a woman spooks a man is to be at her worst when his guard is up and his sensitivity to danger is most keen. This occurs when he's meeting you or on your first dates. If you wondered why he didn't call back, it's because you probably "spooked" him.

YOU HOOK HIM WHEN HIS GUARD IS DOWN: You hook a man when his guard is down and you're at your best. If he catches a glimpse of you in action doing your thing and being yourself, that's the time he finds himself naturally adoring you. For many men, falling in love is easier from the safety of a little distance than by being up close and under pressure.

WHAT MAKES HIM CALL BACK INITIALLY: If you avoid spooking him early and from a distance he starts to adore you, then what makes him call you back is the filling of a starving emotional hunger (refer to page 205).

WHAT MAKES HIM CALL BACK REPEATEDLY: In order to get him to call you back after his initial starving needs have been satisfied is your ability to keep him fascinated with your woman's wiggle (see page 164). Your seamless blending of your five feminine modes of the Boss, Saint, Mom, Pal, and Playmate are what he never tires of and also what he can't get enough of.

LAND HIM WITH THE TRIPLE HOOK: In order to land the big fish in a committed love relationship, you must set a deep emotional, physical, and, most importantly, spiritual hook inside his soul. When he says to himself, "She's the one!" then it's time to ease him into your net. For him the safety and comfort of your loving net is far superior and compelling than swimming around in the social world aimlessly.

*The Bottom Line: Spook him when he's on-guard and you're at your worst.
Hook him when he's off-guard and you're at your best.
Land him with a secure emotional, physical, and spiritual attachment.

How to Catch a Man Off-Guard

"The master social skill is putting others at ease."
—Steve Nakamoto

I believe that the essence of falling in love is simply this: You spook 'em away when their guard is up and you're at your worst. You hook 'em good when their guard is down and you're at your best. You must hook 'em before you spook 'em otherwise you'll lose 'em. Remember, men are like fish and frightened fish (men) can't be caught. Here are a few tips for getting a man to lower his guard so that he can be more vulnerable to your absolute best:

HAVE HIM OBSERVE YOU FROM A DISTANCE: Engage in activities that allow you to perform at your best while letting the man observe, admire, and appreciate you in the safety of his own space. If you're at a party, he'll notice how well others respond to you from the other side of the room as social proof that you're someone special.

GET HIM TO LAUGH AT HIMSELF: Poking a little fun at a man without offending him is a delicate art. This is done in private or only with a small group of his best friends in a light-hearted situation. But whatever you do, avoid a public embarrassment or humiliation at all costs.

DON'T TAKE YOURSELF TOO SERIOUSLY: Showing a lighter side of you and your own vulnerability makes it easier for a man to do likewise. If you tend to be too serious, then mix in a little humor. And on the other hand, if you tend to be too silly, then toss in a little more seriousness.

BE BRUTALLY HONEST IN SMALL DOSES: Show that you're down-to-earth and not too weak by adding small doses of brutal honesty. This shows that you're not a phony, but a person with real feelings. Leading with a bit of candor allows the other person to let go of some similar thoughts.

GET HIM TO LIGHTEN UP: If you sense that a man feels uncomfortable about a question you asked or a topic under discussion, be quick to say that it's no big deal, there's no right or wrong, or simply change the subject. Men can often be afraid of the natural reactions of women and would rather not say anything than to cause an upset or negative evaluation.

DON'T CONFUSE POLITENESS WITH CONSENT: While politeness is often regarded as a sign of respect, be sure to realize that it may also signal that the person is dealing very cautiously with you. As a way of not offending or disappointing you, a man may politely agree or comply with you, but in the future he may feel uncomfortable and avoid you as much as possible.

IT'S ALL ABOUT FEELING COMFORTABLE: For a man, the woman he loves is the one he's happily willing to share all his deepest emotional secrets with. That woman makes him feel safe from excessive judgement and gives him the peace of mind to be himself naturally.

*The Bottom Line: Master the skill of putting others at ease and making them feel more comfortable with you. It will lead to more friends and deeper love connections. Comfort and trust go hand-in-hand with intimacy and love.

The Seven Emotional Hungers

"He liked to observe emotions; they were like red
lanterns strung along the dark unknown of
another's personality, marking vulnerable points."
—Ayn Rand
Author of *Atlas Shrugged* (1957)

There are basic human emotions that all people need in order to feel happy and fulfilled. If a person is undernourished in any of these emotions, they will tend to gravitate toward those who can fill these needs most elegantly. When a frustrated angler finds herself faced with a fish (man) that won't bite, it may be because he gets his hungers filled from outside sources. Here are seven key emotions that men hunger for in their love lives:

THE HUNGER FOR STABILITY: One of the main reasons that a man will seek a more mature woman is the stability, security, and peace of mind that she brings to a relationship. In an uncertain world, it is the feeling of certainty that is often most highly prized.

THE HUNGER FOR SURPRISE: A younger woman is often appealing to an older man because of the surprise and delight that she brings to a love relationship. While certainty is highly prized, so is a little uncertainty to create excitement, variety, and spontaneity in a man's life.

THE HUNGER FOR APPRECIATION: A man hungers to be recognized for his unique qualities, achievements, or gifts. It is by being sincerely appreciated by a woman that a man feels special and significant as a human being.

THE HUNGER FOR BELONGING: Deep inside a man's heart must be a feeling that he really belongs with her. While he may enjoy the feeling of being unique or significant as an individual, he also needs to feel the special connection of being a vital part of her inner circle.

THE HUNGER FOR A COMPELLING FUTURE: For love to last, there must be growth. A man hungers for a woman who he clearly feels will be a major part of creating a brighter and more exciting future for him.

THE HUNGER TO GIVE: Real love involves both giving and receiving. A man hungers for the woman he can please by receiving his emotional gifts with honest delight and gratitude. Like a great performer, a man is inspired to greatness by a woman who is a warm and appreciative audience.

THE HUNGER TO FEEL GRATEFUL: A man who feels the magic of true love rarely obsesses about the benefits and trade-offs with a woman. Instead he is simply grateful for having this particular woman appear in his life. The greatest need for a man is the need to get down on his knees and thank the heavens for being blessed with the love of a woman he adores and cherishes.

* The Bottom Line: Create an unshakable attachment by consistently filling a man's greatest emotional hungers. Become the unique source that leads a man to deeper feelings of happiness, fulfillment, joy, and peace of mind.

Anger Management For Anglers

"Stop looking at the opposite sex as the enemy."
—Abby Hirsch, syndicated columnist

If you want to be cherished by a man, the simplest way is to understand and appreciate him first. You will then be in a better position to be cherished by him in return. To help you maintain a resourceful emotional state, here are some tips on how to keep your upsets to a bare minimum:

IF IT WASN'T INTENTIONAL, THEN YOU ONLY GET TO BE SLIGHT-LY ANNOYED: People sometimes do or say things that inadvertently hurt another person. Give the person a break because of a lack of intent to harm.

IF IT WASN'T EXCESSIVE, THEN YOU ONLY GET TO BE A BIT PEEV-ED: People may also do or say something a few insignificant times that cause pain. But if they realize the effects of their actions, they will often cut out their unwanted behavior. Give some slack if their painful act was only occasional.

IF IT WASN'T INAPPROPRIATE, THEN YOU ONLY GET TO FEEL SLIGHTLY BELOW AVERAGE: Sometimes a painful action is merited because it was meant to prevent a greater or more lasting pain. In this case, the action may be warranted because in its proper context it was appropriate.

HOWEVER, IF THE HURTFUL ACT WAS ALL THREE (INTENTIONAL, EXCES-SIVE, AND INAPPROPRIATE), THEN YOU DO THE FOLLOWING:

1) **FRAME YOUR INTENT IN ADVANCE:** Tell him that in a moment you're going to share something that may hurt short-term, but it is the right thing to do in order to maintain your long-term trust in him.

2) **ASK PERMISSION TO SHARE:** With respect to him, say that you will only share what you mean to say after he's given you permission. Tell him that you don't want to catch him off-guard and make this seem any more painful than it actually is.

3) **WAIT FOR HIS PERMISSION:** If you receive permission, follow up by asking, "are you sure?" If not, say "when you're ready, I'm ready."

4) **STATE YOUR POSITION CLEARLY:** Start by saying "what you did was unfair to me as a person." Pause and then state your position clearly and suc-cinctly. Then state what you need from him instead (Hint: make it easy).

5) **STOP THE BATTLE:** If you find yourself starting to drift into the neg-ative, stop immediately and end the conversation by saying, "All I can say is I'm not angry, I'm just disappointed. I know you're a better man than that."

* Note: **Discipline your disappointment when the stakes are minor, but be strong when the consequences are major. Quality men will come to respect your display of character when the issues matter and will lighten up when they see that you really don't sweat the small stuff.**

ForeWordReviews.com

5 Star Highest Rating: "An exceptional book"

Most single women have experienced the sinking feeling of fishing for a date from someone special without receiving so much as a nibble. It is enough to make women wonder if there is something wrong with their bait.

Steve Nakamoto, a former Dale Carnegie instructor, personal development trainer, and professional tour director understands these feelings. He has written an intelligent, funny, and wise book for women who are looking to catch a guy—hook, line, and sinker. In this entertaining look at relationships, he compares men to fish who are secretly longing to be caught. Women, on the other hand, are wily yet compassionate anglers looking to reel in the big one.

Men Are Like Fish will take readers on a fact-packed fishing trip where they will learn tips on how to initiate great relationships or enhance the ones they already have. The book is sweetly old-fashioned, yet wickedly on target. Nakamoto has also sprinkled zippy cartoons and unusually helpful quotes throughout the book.

While the title might imply a single-minded effort to drag an unsuspecting man into the net, the book is actually somewhat Zenlike. It will help women to improve their self-images, broaden their interests, and accentuate the unique qualities they possess that will naturally draw good relationships to them. Nakamoto also spends a good deal of time discussing the end of relationships. He shows women how to let go gracefully, with as little pain as possible, so that they can continue to grow without harboring bitterness. He uses several examples from his own life, sharing many of his triumphs and failures with a good-natured sense of humor. Nakamoto shares one especially funny story about a tight jeans contest where he lost a shapely girlfriend/contestant to judge Clint Eastwood. He writes, "I consoled myself with the thought that Deanna must have had a tough choice: Clint Eastwood (People Weekly's 2001 #2 most popular screen actor of all time) or Steve Nakamoto? It could have gone either way, right?"

Nakamoto also shares good, solid advice. One especially helpful area is "Favorite Fishing Holes: 101 Hot Spots Where the Big Ones Are Biting." It consists of a list of fun and inexpensive activities and places to explore that are bound to be interesting, even if they do not spark a new love affair. Among the many activities that Nakamoto recommends are going to art gallery openings, visiting wineries for wine tasting and tours, and taking city tours or day trips in one's own city or in a nearby town.

Nakamoto does not guarantee eternal love for readers. However, both single women looking for that perfect catch and those seeking to recapture the romance of an exciting relationship will find great value here. *Men Are Like Fish* is guaranteed to give even the most jaded and discouraged romantic angler a new, more joyful perspective on the oldest sport in the world. — Reviewed by Kathleen Youman

FREE
SPECIAL REPORT

- The Complete "Favorite Fishing Holes" Report
- Find Out Where The Big Ones Are Biting Near You
- Over 280 Favorite Fishing Holes In 7 Categories
- 40 Hot Spots Where "Rich Fish" Are Biting
- 10 New Tips For Successful Online Dating
- Over 20 Pages of Lists, Tests, and Simple Exercises

To receive your free copy, send an email request to:

tips@menarelikefish.com